A Squirrel
of One's Own

Books by Douglas Fairbairn

A Man's World
The Voice of Charlie Pont
A Gazelle on the Lawn
A Squirrel of One's Own

A Squirrel of One's Own

Douglas Fairbairn

The McCall Publishing Company

NEW YORK

Published simultaneously in Canada by
Doubleday Canada Ltd., Toronto

Library of Congress Catalog Card Number: 72-122123

ISBN 0-8415-0121-1

The McCall Publishing Company
230 Park Avenue
New York, N.Y. 10017

PRINTED IN THE UNITED STATES OF AMERICA

Design by Tere LoPrete

PART ONE

One

This is the way these things always begin. You happen to be in a certain place at a certain time—strolling through the woods or through a park or along a beach or even across a vacant lot, or just standing in your back yard smoking a cigarette, or looking absently out of a window at the clouds or the trees or the clothes on a clothesline blowing in the wind—when an unexpected movement catches your eye or you hear a mysterious sound, and suddenly you are alert, watching, listening, knowing intuitively that something special is happening or is about to happen right there in front of you.

On the evening of July 7, 1965, I was standing gazing out of a window of a house that is situated on an exotically foliaged piece of land overlooking a wide bay on the east coast of Florida, where I lived then and still do now.

It was dusk. The air was hot and still. It was the dry season between the wet seasons in late spring and early fall and I suppose I was just standing there wishing that I would hear distant thunder and feel a breeze from the Everglades with the smell of rain in it spring up, I don't know. Anyway, I was about to turn from the window when I happened to see a cat emerge from the underbrush across the lawn and come loping in my direction. Even in that light and at that distance I could tell from the way it moved and held its head that it was bringing back alive some bit of game that it had just caught out among the trees. Probably a lizard or a mouse, I thought. The cat held its head high and bounded delicately over the fallen coconuts and palm fronds in its way. It was in a hurry, but it was being very careful too not to jar loose its prize from its jaws as it ran. As it came closer I saw that it was Bella, one of the large number of neighborhood cats that seemed to spend most of their time living and loving right below my windows.

I knew what Bella had on her mind. She had recently had a new batch of kittens and she intended to use the mouse or whatever it was as a teaching aid to try to drive some of the hard realities of a cat's life into their silly heads. The kittens, wide-eyed and playful but still unweaned, were lolling on the grass down below me, while nearby some full-grown cats lounged about, yawning and washing their paws.

The instant the kittens saw their mother approaching they jumped up and ran toward her, stumbling over themselves and each other in their eagerness to get to her. But when they saw that she was carrying something in her mouth they stopped dead in their tracks. I still couldn't see clearly what it was that Bella was carrying, but it looked about the size of a mouse and I was pretty sure that that was what it was. Again, I started to turn away from the window. I knew very well what was going to happen next. Bella would put the mouse down on the ground and pretend to let it go. The mouse would make a run for it, but before it got very far Bella would pounce on it, rake it in, toss it in the air a few times, worry it a little, pretend to let it go again, then pounce on it again, over and over. The kittens would watch, spellbound. The other cats would come to life and fan out behind Bella and start creeping up on her with their bellies brushing the ground, looking for an opening to dart in and snatch her mouse away from her.

But I hesitated. I saw Bella put the mouse down on the grass. She held it down with her right paw. The kittens edged closer to her. The other cats had already stirred and sniffed the air. Bella lifted her paw, and I—we all—held our breath, waiting for the mouse to make a break for it. But it didn't move. It was very small. To me it seemed no more than a little ball of dust on the grass. When, after a decent interval, the mouse still didn't move, Bella reached out and gave it a tentative cuff with her paw. Still nothing happened. Bella gazed at the mouse for a moment and then suddenly rolled her head to one side, flattened her ears, planted her back feet wide apart, and dealt it a couple of lightning-fast, stiff-armed jabs that were plainly meant to convey to it the idea that she wanted it to do something very dramatic and she wanted it to start doing it right away. Then she stood back a little, her tail lashing furiously, and waited. I waited too, fascinated in spite of myself, and telling myself as always when this was going on that the cats were only doing their job when they caught mice and that if they ever stopped I would be overrun in no time. And yet I felt sorry for the mouse and wished that just this once anyway it could be different and somehow this one would outwit the cats and escape from them unharmed.

A moment passed. Well, good then, I thought, Bella had given the mouse a fatal nip by mistake when she had caught it, and she either didn't realize that it was dead yet or was just too proud to admit it even to herself. So it was over, and there would not have to be any cruel games after all.

But just then Bella gave the mouse another quick tap with her paw and this time it did move. The trouble was that instead of trying to get away from Bella it crawled a couple of inches toward her. Thoroughly startled, Bella jumped backwards, but then the mouse crawled a couple of more inches toward her. Bella didn't know what to make of it. She started to bat the mouse again and changed her mind and started again and hesitated. She moved a little to the left and then a little to the right, trying to get a look at the impertinent creature from different angles. Finally she turned a complete circle and sat down, swaying slightly on her haunches, only the tip of her tail twitching now, and there was a long pause.

Then all of a sudden the mouse launched itself toward Bella again, and this time it not only succeeded in reaching her but actually squeezed itself in between her front legs and fetched up right against her belly. This was too much for Bella. She leaped up and withdrew to a safe distance and stood there looking embarrassed, skeptical and apprehensive.

At that point I went outside to get a better view of this peculiar mouse. The light was very bad by then. I was standing on a balcony and I leaned over the balustrade and for the first time I could see that for a mouse this mouse had a very strange-looking tail indeed. It was not the shoelace that it should have been but a long silvery feather laid out on the grass. In that instant, I realized that the only thing the mouse could be with a tail like that was a baby squirrel, and I also realized that I would have to do everything I possibly could to rescue it from Bella. My first impulse was to run down the steps as fast as I could, yelling wildly, waving my arms and clapping my hands, hoping that if I got down there fast enough and made enough noise on the way the cat would be so alarmed that it would just run off and leave the squirrel where it was. But I restrained myself. I had had a certain amount of experience in the past of trying to save birds from these cats, and I knew that at the first bark out of me the odds were that Bella would grab up the squirrel and beat it to the nearest bushes and that would be the end of it. My only real hope was to sneak up on her, but there wasn't much time left for that. At any moment Bella might decide to execute the squirrel out of sheer frustration or one of the other cats might catch her off guard and snap it up and run.

I went quietly down the steps to the terrace and stood under a trellis covered with bougainvillaea. I could see the cats through the leaves and the dark red flowers but they couldn't see me. The status quo remained. The kittens sat in a row watching their mother, the squirrel lay still on the grass, Bella stood nervously off a little way, the big cats hovered in the background.

I went down the remaining steps and all of the cats looked at me as I started walking slowly toward Bella. I only had a short distance to go. All of a sudden the kittens scuttled for the jasmine bush nearby that was always their hiding place when they thought they were in danger. At the same time, Bella moved forward swiftly and crouched over the squirrel, her mouth poised above the nape of its neck and her front paws boxing it in. I talked to her softly as I walked. She made one move as if

7

to grab up the squirrel but didn't, and then I was there, standing over them. I had realized from the beginning that if I succeeded in getting close enough to the cat and the squirrel to try to take the one from the other, the chances were marvelous that the cat would bite me. As it turned out, when I reached down the cat just turned away, but the squirrel bit me. It wasn't a serious bite. It didn't break the skin or hurt much and all the squirrel really meant by it, I think, was to let me know that although it was very small and a little weak at the moment I wasn't to get the idea that it was completely defenseless. That point having been made, it curled itself around my thumb so tightly that there was no question at all of my having to hold onto it to keep it from falling as I stood up and lifted it off the grass. I held up my thumb and looked at it for a minute. It was unbelievable. A baby squirrel was curled around it. It didn't move and it didn't seem to have any weight at all, but it felt soft and surprisingly warm. So, holding my thumb up in front of me and moving with a solemn tread, I went back across the grass, up the first flight of steps, under the trellis, across the terrace, up the next flight of steps to the balcony, opened the door and took the squirrel into my house.

Two

I went into the bedroom and knelt by the bed and lowered my hand until it rested on the bed. The squirrel didn't move. I couldn't even feel it breathing. But it was holding on hard. I couldn't see where it began or ended because it had wound its tail completely around itself and it looked like nothing but a ring of gray fur on my thumb. I waited a few minutes, hoping it would at least lift its tail and take a quick look around to see where it was, but nothing happened. Then I thought that perhaps if I cupped my other hand over the squirrel it might begin to feel more secure in the darkness and with the warmth of my hand around it and decide to relax a little. As my hand covered it I felt it give a faint twitch, but that was all, and then for what seemed like a terribly long time there was no further movement whatsoever. Then

I felt the squirrel begin to loosen its grip on my thumb. It let go by degrees, taking such a long time to do it that I was scared I might sneeze or the phone would ring or someone would knock on the door. But finally it let go altogether, and then I could feel it start moving around under my hands. It went in circles, pressing its nose into the cracks between my fingers, and its nose was like velvet. I was dying to look at it but I thought it was best not to move. The squirrel kept turning slowly around and around, exploring my hands, and then suddenly it popped its head up through the space between my thumbs, and for the first time we were face to face.

I had been afraid that when the squirrel realized where it was—in a house, in a room, under a roof, cut off from the trees and the sky—it would either go into shock or start trying frantically to get away from me. But all it did was gaze at me steadily with its big, round, shiny, black, unblinking eyes for a moment. Then it pulled itself the rest of the way up out of the hollow of my hands.

I had never seen a baby squirrel before. In fact I had never touched a squirrel of any age or seen one up that close. It sat up on top of my hands and just kept on looking at me for a while, and it felt strange to be stared at so directly, candidly and unblinkingly. I had no idea how old it was but I thought it couldn't have been more than two weeks old. It was about three inches long, not counting its tail, which was roughly of an equal length. It was light gray all over except for its underside, which from its chin back to the base of its tail and inside its legs was pure white. The line between the white and the gray was very clearly drawn. Its ears were only little buds pressed flat against the sides of its head, and its tail had not yet even begun to look like the classic bush of the grown squirrel; instead the long silvery hairs lay flat along its tail and tapered to a point at the end, like the hairs of a watercolor brush.

Abruptly, it turned away from me and skidded down the back of my hand head foremost, letting its back claws drag across my skin behind it as brakes. Its claws were needle-sharp like a kitten's, but I noticed that they weren't retractable like a cat's. It started exploring the backs of my hands just as it had the palms, searching in every crack and fold of them with its nose. I tried to catch its attention by speaking to it in a whisper, but the only thing about me that really seemed to interest it was my hands.

I tried to pick it up and hold it. I wanted to examine it to see if it was hurt in any way. I figured that what had happened was that it had fallen from its nest and Bella had come across it in the course of her regular afternoon mouse-and-lizard hunt. Since it could have fallen thirty or forty feet from an oak or a coconut palm and then had been carried across a field in a cat's mouth and subsequently given a good pasting by the same cat, I didn't see how it could possibly have escaped some kind of injury. But it was impossible to hold onto it for more than a second because it didn't want to be held and its body was so supple that it flowed away through my fingers like water.

It kept crawling all over my hands, nuzzling them frantically, and finally it hit me like a bolt out of the blue: It was looking for milk. My hands were warm just as its mother had been warm and warmth meant milk. And that was why it had been chasing after Bella so determinedly too. I began to feel a little dizzy then, realizing that this squirrel was going to have to get fed very soon if it wasn't going to die of starvation and I was going to have to be the one who did the feeding. It wasn't my sort of thing. I wasn't good in baby situations or life and death situations. I didn't know what to feed it. Milk? That was too easy. There would have to be something in the milk. What? And would a baby squirrel lap up milk from a bowl anyway? No matter what you added to it? Of course not! I knew that there would have to be an eyedropper involved in it somewhere. There was always an eyedropper involved in these things somewhere. I didn't think I had an eyedropper.

What I wished at that moment was that I could have handed over the squirrel to someone right then who would have known exactly what to do with it. But I didn't know anyone like that. The people I knew would have felt just as helpless and incompetent as I did. You're always reading in the paper about people who have brought home baby raccoons or blue jays or something and are doing first-class jobs of raising them, but the only times I or anyone I ever knew had tried to save a wild animal or a bird the poor thing invariably had been found dead in its pathetic little box in the kitchen by the stove the next morning. I was full of pessimism. Already I could see the squirrel dead. Already I could see myself finding a shoebox to put it in, carrying it across the field, burying it in the shade under the oaks.

Then it occurred to me to call the Humane Society. I got a pillow and put it in the middle of the bed and made a hollow under it. When I put the squirrel into the hollow it started burrowing deeper into it and while it was busy doing that I thought I would have time to make my call.

A girl answered the telephone and was quick to say that she was sorry but the Humane Society was closed for the day. I told her my story anyway—how I had found a baby squirrel and it was starving and all I wanted was to have someone tell me what to feed it and how.

"Squirrels are wild animals, sir," the girl said, in a

weary tone, as if she went through this same thing thousands of times a day and was damn tired of it.

"I know that," I said.

"Sir," she said, "you are not allowed to keep, or own, or possess any sort of wild animal in the state of Florida. All wild animals in the state of Florida are protected by the state of Florida. To keep, or own, or possess them is against the law and you could be prosecuted. Put the squirrel back where you found it, sir. The mother knows it's missing. She will come and get it. As a matter of fact, she's probably out looking for it right now."

"There's just one little problem," I said. "Where I found this squirrel was between the two front paws of a big cat that was about to eat it up."

"A cat?" the girl said.

"A cat."

"Is it hurt?"

"I don't think so," I said. "I can't say for sure, but it doesn't seem to have any broken bones anyway. Its eyes are bright. Its nose is cold. It's a little wobbly on its legs, but then, as I told you, it's starving."

"Well, the only thing it's going to take is milk," the girl said, changing her tone completely. "Warm up some milk and put a little sugar in it and give it to the squirrel with an eyedropper."

"I don't think I have an eyedropper."

"Well, look around. You've got one somewhere. Everybody's got one somewhere. What about tomorrow?"

"What do you mean?"

"Will you be able to go on taking care of it? It will want to get fed about every four or five hours for maybe a couple of weeks. Will you be able to handle that?"

"I don't think so."

"Have to go to work, huh? Away all day, huh?"

"Well, it isn't that so much," I said. "Actually, I work

right here at home. It's just that I really don't feel—well, I'm really just not the type for this sort of—I just don't really want to get all that much involved in something like this."

"Uhuh. Nobody around there who can take over for you?"

"No one."

"Uhuh. Sir, you say you took this squirrel away from a cat, right?"

"Right."

"And you have no idea where the cat found it in the first place, right?"

"Right."

"Well, then you can't very well go out tomorrow morning and stick it somewhere where the mother would probably come along and find it, can you? So somebody's going to have to be taking care of it until it can make it on its own, right? Do you want to bring it over here tomorrow?"

"You'll take care of it?"

"That's what we're supposed to be here for, isn't it? And when it's ready to go, we'll take it out in the woods somewhere and let it go."

"That sounds fair enough to me," I said. "I'll be there first thing in the morning."

I hung up and reached into the hollow under the pillow to see what the squirrel was up to. It seemed to be all right so I left it there and went into the bathroom and looked around desperately for an eyedropper. As the girl had said, everybody has one somewhere, and I found one in an old bottle of dried-up eye drops in the medicine cabinet. I squirted some warm water through it to rinse it out, checked on the squirrel again and then went out to the kitchen and began warming up some milk. I put a little sugar in it, as I had been instructed, and thought I was doing pretty well. But then, as I stood there stirring the milk, my awful feeling of pessimism returned. I remembered the blue jay I had tried to nurse back to health once. I had managed to make the cat that had caught it cough it up by rapping it smartly over the top of the head with a stick. The bird was hurt, but I tried my best to pull it through. For one thing, I have a great fondness for blue jays. They're such a wonderful blue, if they were rare, people would go a long way just to catch a glimpse of one. I tried as hard as I could to make the bird take the mashed banana, mashed apple, and bits of raw hamburger that the lady at the Audubon Society had told me over the telephone to feed it, but I failed, and the next morning I found it dead, still with a little of the unwanted mashed banana on its bill.

The squirrel would die too, I thought. No matter how carefully I warmed its milk and patiently tried to feed it from the eyedropper, it would not eat, and in the morning I would go to look at it and it would be dead.

The milk was ready. I took the saucepan and the eyedropper into the bedroom and got the squirrel out from under the pillow. With my right hand I filled the eyedropper and with my left took hold of the squirrel and tried to bring the two together. At first I had no luck at all, but then I grasped the squirrel firmly and turned it over on its back, and for a moment it stopped its wriggling, just long enough for me to squeeze a couple of drops of the warm milk from the eyedropper onto its mouth. The effect was astonishing. The squirrel reached for the tip of the eyedropper with both paws, seized it with a death grip, stuck it in its mouth, and started sucking on it as if it had been taking its milk that way for years. Loud smacking accompanied the sucking. There was a lot of slobbering too and soon the squirrel's face and chest and paws were soaking wet. I was very happy.

My pessimism went straight out the window. The squirrel kept getting more excited and the smacking got louder and louder. Then all of a sudden it lost the tip of the eyedropper, and instead of letting me give it back to it, it started wildly trying to find it itself. I kept sticking the tip right in front of its nose and it kept knocking it out of the way in its eagerness to find it again. It searched blindly, as if it turned off its eyes altogether in order to concentrate on scent, trying to smell it out with its nose alone. Unfortunately, the system didn't work too well. The squirrel kept running into the eyedropper and sailing right on past it and then getting more excited than ever and running off in nine different directions at once to try to find it again. Finally it got the tip back into its mouth again, but then I saw that the eyedropper was empty. The squirrel held on fiercely when I tried to take it away from it, but I got it loose and filled it up again, and the squirrel happily went back to its smacking and slobbering.

After it had polished off four or five eyedroppersful of milk, the squirrel suddenly relaxed and didn't want anything more to do with the eyedropper. Its behavior had changed remarkably. Before it hadn't wanted to be still for an instant. Now it sat in my palm and yawned. It had become very drowsy. I dried off its face and chest and paws with the corner of a towel and it submitted to that without any fuss at all. As soon as I was through it curled up in my palm, pulled its tail over its eyes, and went sound asleep. I put my other hand over it and sat there for a while wondering what to do next. Finally I put a towel into the handiest thing around at the moment—a yellow beach bag—put the squirrel into the bag, and covered it with a fold of the towel. It never woke up or even stirred while all this was going on.

I went out somewhere that evening and got back home

around eleven o'clock. I went right over to the beach bag and reached in and pulled the towel apart carefully. The squirrel was curled up in a warm ball and didn't wake up even when I lifted its tail a little to look at its face. Everything was okay except that the towel underneath it was soaked. I got another towel and tried to take the wet one out and put the dry one in without waking up the squirrel. But it did wake up and was ravenously hungry again. I warmed up some more milk and we went through the same performance as before, and then the squirrel went right back to sleep again. I put it back into the beach bag and covered it with the towel and put the bag next to my bed.

Before I turned out my light that night I sat on the side of my bed looking at the beach bag for a long time. I couldn't get over the idea that down inside it a baby squirrel was sleeping very peacefully.

Three

I got up early the next morning, thinking that the sooner I took the squirrel to the Humane Society the better for both of us. The squirrel was still asleep. I had a quick cup of coffee and took a shower and shaved and got dressed. When I looked into the beach bag again I saw that the squirrel hadn't moved. It was still buried in the towel, with just a wisp of tail showing. I opened the blinds and let the sunlight into the room, and then I pulled the towel back and looked at the squirrel. It flicked its tail a couple of times, trying to adjust it to keep the light out of its eyes, but finally it gave up and popped its eyes open.

I fished it out of the beach bag and it sat up in my hands and we surveyed each other again. I had been afraid that the squirrel might have forgotten during its sleep everything that had happened the evening before and that when it woke up and saw where it was it would go into shock. But it just sat in my hands smelling the breeze coming through the windows and listening to the birds splashing in the birdbath down on the terrace. I was looking at it, thinking how handsome it was with the sunlight glistening on its fur, when suddenly it began the wild nuzzling of my hands that meant it was famished again.

I warmed up the milk and fed the squirrel, thinking that it was for the last time and feeling sad about it because now that I had learned how to do it—in fact, had really gotten very good at it—I thought it was fantastic fun. I liked the whole routine—watching the squirrel grab the bottle and stick it in its mouth, listening to the smacking, even the final drying off of the face and chest and paws. And there was something about feeding the squirrel that appealed to me on another level too, the idea that its life was in my hands and it knew it and trusted me.

I made sure the squirrel took all the milk it could handle. I wanted it to be stuffed because I thought it would go right back to sleep as usual as soon as it was full, and I was nervous about the car ride to the Humane Society and wanted it to sleep all the way there if possible. My plan was to put the squirrel into the beach bag the minute it fell asleep and to drive it to the Humane Society as fast as I could and hand it over to them beach bag and all, hoping that it wouldn't wake up so that I wouldn't have to look at it again and say good-bye or anything.

But this time the squirrel didn't want to go to sleep immediately after it had gotten through gorging itself. It let me give it a quick clean-up, but then it slipped out of my hands, dropped into my lap and started creeping along my thigh toward my knee.

Its movements were painfully slow and cautious. It kept low, with its hindquarters flattened and its belly dragging along my thigh. It carried its tail pointing forward and floating over its back and neck defensively, and I could feel its claws sticking through my pants leg like little fishhooks, clinging to me. It inched along, its head swaying from side to side, and sometimes bobbing up and down, and you would have thought it was threading its way through a whole jungleful of cats and owls. When it reached my knee it stretched out with its back legs straddling my leg and its claws hooked firmly into my pants, and it was absolutely still, not even seeming to breathe.

It was hard to see how any living thing could stay so still for such a long time. Minutes passed and there was no movement whatsoever, not even the slightest twitch of a whisker. The squirrel's beautiful tail lay flat along my leg now. Its silky fur, in the sun, didn't look plain gray any longer but flecked with gold, green, copper, blue, silver, purple, brown, and red.

The longer the squirrel lay so still, the more I worried about the same thing I had worried about the evening before, that a sudden noise might produce a violent reaction from it. For my part, I tried to be as still as I could, not breathing too hard, not scratching any of the dozens of places that seemed to be crying out for a good scratching. I kept thinking how lucky I was that I had given up smoking because I knew that if I hadn't I would have been dying for a cigarette right about then—and then, having thought about it too much, I started dying for one anyway.

The birds were making a great racket down on the terrace. In winter the trees around my house attract many species of migrating birds, but now, in midsummer, only the natives were in residence—cardinals, mockingbirds, blue jays, red-bellied woodpeckers and spotted-breasted orioles. But my little squirrel listened to the birds impassively, even when the jays rose to new heights of raucousness. I had wondered what it would do if it heard a squirrel outside and after a while, not far away, I heard one start making the furious *chuck-chuck-chuck* sound that they always make whenever they spy a cat on the prowl in the underbrush. There, I thought, if that isn't an authentic call of the wild, what is? I watched to see what would happen. My squirrel remained impassive. Then it occurred to me that it was only doing what all baby squirrels must do in the morning after breakfast—stretch out on a branch in the sunshine and have a good long think for themselves. And it also occurred to me that whether I liked it or not I had apparently become two very important things to my squirrel—its mother and its tree.

It kept on lying there for quite a while, even letting me stroke its back and nose a little with my finger. But then it must have gotten tired of thinking because it snapped out of it all of a sudden and got up and stretched rather like a cat—yawning wide, arching its back and digging its claws in—and abruptly disappeared over the front of my knee, clearly intending to slide frontwards down my leg to the floor. I didn't think that that was a very good idea and I caught the squirrel halfway down and pulled it loose by plucking its claws off my pants leg one by one, like sandspurs.

I put it on my shoulder and felt it freeze there with its claws digging into my shoulder now, through my shirt. But in a minute it began working its way cautiously toward my ear. When it started exploring my ear with its cold little nose it was excruciating, but when it actually took hold of my ear lobe with its paws and held onto it gently but firmly for about two minutes it was even worse. And then when it pulled the back of my collar aside and stuck its head down the back of my shirt and I felt that cold nose, that velvet face and those bristly whiskers down my neck it was more than anyone could endure and I grew rigid in my chair, my eyes bugged, my feet lifted slightly off the floor and my hands clutched the air like talons. When the squirrel started to go on to my other ear I plucked it off my shoulder and put it down on the bed.

It had a good time exploring the unmade bed, going up hill and down dale like a little tank on rough terrain. While it was doing that I propped myself up on the bed and called a few friends. I told each of them about my squirrel—how I had saved it from the cat, how I had brought it upstairs on my thumb, and how I had gotten to be its mother and its tree.

"Great," they said.

"It really is a beautiful little thing," I said. "And terrific fun to watch. Everything it does is fascinating."

"Are you going to keep it?" they said.

"No."

"Well, what are you going to do with it?"

"As soon as it falls asleep, I'm going to stick it in the car and take it to the Humane Society."

"Isn't that a little mean?" they said.

"I can't help it," I said. "Frankly, I think I've done my part. Now I want the pros to take over."

"I still think it's a little mean," they said. "Here you've been going on for half an hour about how crazy you are about this animal and now you say you're going to turn it over to a bunch of people who couldn't care less about it and who will just treat it as another welfare case."

"That's too bad," I said. "Look, a thing like this is a lot of responsibility. I don't want that kind of responsibility. And it takes a lot of time too, and I don't have any time to spare right now."

"What are you talking about?" they said. "You're a writer, aren't you? All you've got is time to spare. Keep the squirrel for a couple of days—until it gets its strength —and then take it out and put it in one of those colossal oaks you've got down there and it will be grateful to you all the days of its life. You know about Androcles, don't you?"

"I'm not keeping this squirrel," I said.

"That's mean," they said.

While I was on the telephone the squirrel gradually slowed down in its exploration of the bedclothes as it started getting drowsy. Finally it crawled up on my chest, looked around for a place to curl up in, squeezed itself into my left armpit and went to sleep. I was in the middle of a long conversation with someone on a subject completely unrelated to squirrels when I felt a wave of great warmth flowing down my left side. I said good-bye quickly, hung up, and reached in and removed the limp squirrel from my armpit. I was appalled. I couldn't figure out how anything that small could produce such a deluge. It went right on sleeping angelically as I carried it over to the beach bag, put it down inside and covered it with the towel. I took another shower and put on another shirt. Then I returned to the bedroom and stood looking at the beach bag.

The squirrel was still asleep. The moment I had been waiting for had come.

I had to face the fact that there really no longer was any question of my taking the squirrel to the Humane Society. Perhaps there never had been. Anyway, I knew that nothing could have made me pick up that beach bag with the squirrel sleeping in it and carry it out the door.

I sat down and tried to think clearly about the situation. I decided that I would keep the squirrel until it went off milk and began eating real food. Then I would take it out one fine morning, stick it in an oak tree, tell it good-bye and that would be that. I felt much better then. The whole thing, I imagined, would probably turn out to be a very pleasant and perhaps even educational little interlude that I would always look back on with great fondness.

Around eleven o'clock that morning the squirrel woke up and I gave it another feeding. That was when it occurred to me that I ought to find out whether it was a boy or a girl. So when it was through stuffing itself I turned it over on its back and had a look. There really was very little to go on, and you had to pull apart a lot of fluff back there to see what little there was. But I decided it was a girl. I felt good about that because that was what I had hoped it was. Then I thought she should have a name. So I named her Chippy.

Four

When I was a freshman at Harvard I lived in a spectacu-
larly homely dormitory in the Yard called Matthews
Hall. My room was on the fifth floor and there was almost
nothing good about it. It was cold and drafty and
creaked, but the worst part was the isolation. Nobody
ever wanted to come around to see you because they were
damned if they were going to climb five steep flights of
stairs for anybody. The most they would do was stand
below your window and howl your name. And you had a
tendency to want to stay in your room once you got
there, only going out for essentials—lectures, meals and
football games. But there was one good thing. Up there
so high, I was on a level with the topmost branches of the
trees in the Yard and when I got tired of studying I
could always stand at my window and watch the squirrels.

I got to be a great fan of the Yard squirrels and I smuggled tons of bread to them from the Union that winter after the snow came. When the bells started ringing between classes they would come down to the ground, hoping that of the hundreds of students crossing back and forth in the Yard a few might have a crust of bread or a couple of peanuts in their pockets for them, and I never could resist their worried little faces.

After that year I lost touch with squirrels for a long time, but many years later when I came here to this house to live and found that the trees around it were full of squirrels, my interest in them was renewed. What struck me first was that although there is a great deal of difference between the ecology of Massachusetts and of tropical Florida, the squirrels here looked very much like the ones I had known in Harvard Yard. One day I looked up squirrels at the library in the village. All I could find was a short article on them in the Brittanica, but from it I learned that the reason these squirrels looked so much like the Yard squirrels was that they were of the very same species—*sciurus carolinensis,* or Eastern gray squirrel.

I had never bothered to try to read up on squirrels until that day and I never tried again—until Chippy came into my life. Then I wanted to find out everything there was to know. I went back to the library and made a more thorough search this time, but still all I could find was a couple of short articles here and there that were not very informative. Piecing it all together, this is what it amounted to. Gray squirrels are common in the entire eastern half of the United States. They mate twice a year and produce two litters of between three and five babies. The gestation period is forty-four days. The babies are born blind and naked, and they mature very slowly in comparison to most other mammals. For the first three or four weeks of their lives they are completely helpless, and the mother must remain with them almost continuously during that time to feed them and to protect them from rain and cold and predators. The fur comes on the baby squirrels in patches and they don't get full fur until they are about a month old. They start venturing out of the nest after they get full fur, but they are not weaned until they are two months old and they are not fully mature until they are two years old.

From that I gathered that Chippy was at least a month old, but I didn't think she could be much more than that because she was not very strong and was still taking milk.

When I came back from the library I took a walk around the property, trying to figure out what tree Chippy might have fallen from. I remembered a coconut palm in which I had seen a squirrel hard at work building a nest one afternoon not long before. I went and stood at the base of the palm and looked up. I could see the nest up there, above the clusters of ripening coconuts, held fast in the angle between two fronds. The nest was made of the feathery twigs of a royal poinciana, some of whose branches passed through the palm's fronds. The squirrel had woven the twigs into a hollow ball about half the size of a basketball. The entrance was a small hole that opened onto the wide trough of the lower frond. The nest was about twenty feet off the ground. A long fall, I thought. But it could have been much worse; there were other coconut palms nearby that were much taller, and I had seen nests in the oaks that could have been fifty feet off the ground.

I walked around and looked up at all of the nests that I knew the locations of, but it was futile. There was no way of knowing which one Chippy had fallen from. I saw a lot of squirrels. Some were working in the fruit trees, others were digging up and burying things in the dry leaves on the ground, and a few were just chasing each other through the high branches or around and around the massive trunks of the oaks.

It was another hot July day, but there was a good breeze coming up the slope from the bay, and it was quite cool in the shade of the trees. As I walked back toward my house I thought—as I had so many times before —that this place really was a sort of heaven on earth for squirrels. Here the ground never froze, the snows never came, the icy wind never bit, and there was such a great variety of trees—sapodilla, ficus, jacaranda, live oak, gumbo limbo, ironwood, banana, coconut, lime, lemon, orange, grapefruit, poinciana, woman's tongue, mango, holly, golden shower, cannonball, cottonwood—that there never was a time when all of them were bare at once (and most of them never were), and also never a time when they were not producing acorns, nuts, seeds, and fruit in abundance.

I paused to watch two squirrels playing in the leaves around the base of an oak, but then I hurried on, remembering that I had a squirrel of my own in the house and that it was getting close to her feeding time.

Five

One afternoon only three days after Chippy had come to live with me something ominous happened. I came home and as I entered the bedroom I saw a blur of silver and gray streak across the rug and dive headfirst into the beach bag. Chippy had been under the bureau. When I fished her out of the beach bag she had little balls of dust on her nose and tail and whiskers and she looked pleased with herself. That made me stop and think.

In the first place she was supposed to have been asleep at that hour, and in the second place I had prevented her from going under the bureau enough times for her to know that it was strictly off-limits to her. The thing I had to face squarely was that from now on she was going to have to be contained somehow when I wasn't around to watch her because obviously the time was past when I could feed her and put her to bed in the beach bag and expect her to sleep for four or five hours. I had seen it coming. Each day she had been getting steadily bolder and quicker and stronger and wanted to sleep less and play with me and explore the house more. It was amazing how fast she was changing from a helpless infant into a very active, curious, and increasingly self-confident young animal. And I should say rebellious too, because I had already observed that when I kept her from going some-where—like under the bureau—from then on that was all she had on her mind.

I was afraid that if she started roaming around on her own she might crawl under something and get stuck or fall from somewhere and break a leg or find some old ant poison or a roach tablet and take a nibble of it.

The only thing I could find on the spur of the moment to use as a cage was a plastic laundry basket. I got it out of the closet and set it upside down in the middle of the floor in the bedroom. Chippy approached it warily but purposefully, as she did every strange object that looked as if it might be a threat to her. When she got close enough to the basket to sniff it, I lifted it up and put it down over her. There, I thought, the problem was solved as easy as that. The basket was an excellent cage. The openings were too small for Chippy to slip through but they were big enough for us to see each other and for me to stick my fingers in and wiggle them at her.

But Chippy didn't share my enthusiasm. She seemed to know immediately that the basket was a cage and that a cage is a jail and that a jail is a bad place to be on the inside looking out of. She had four little teeth, two on the top and two on the bottom, and she made a quick tour of the inside perimeter of the basket, pausing every few inches to gnaw at the plastic bars, looking for weak spots.

I was relieved to see that her teeth made no impression on the plastic. I knew that they would get sharper and stronger but my theory was that by the time she was able to gnaw her way out of the basket it would be time for her to go back to the trees anyway.

I had barely finished congratulating myself on my ingenuity when Chippy sprang herself. It was hard to believe, but I had looked away for an instant and when I looked back there she was scooting across the rug toward the bureau and all that great dust under it that she liked getting herself covered with so much. I swooped down and caught her and brought her back and put her under the basket again, and then I watched to see how she did it. Without hesitation she ran to one of the two narrow slits at the ends of the basket, through which you were meant to stick your fingers when you picked up the basket, flattened herself down remarkably, squeezed through the slit, and escaped.

There was no getting around it, in this business quick thinking was everything. If you couldn't improvise on the spot you were lost. I put Chippy back under the basket and grabbed a pair of Japanese sandals and wedged the toes of them into the slots. Chippy went right to work gnawing at the sandals and trying desperately to nudge them out of the way with her nose, but everything failed. She seemed to grow more and more desperate as the realization sank in that she was definitely trapped this time. She went back to running around and around the perimeter of the cage gnawing at the bars, but after a while she saw how futile it was and she stopped and just stood looking at me. I didn't feel so smart then because I knew she was thinking that I had played a pretty rotten trick on her. I tried to make up to her by letting her out from under the basket and playing with her for a long time.

Then I gave her a feeding and when she started getting drowsy I put her to bed in the beach bag and put the laundry basket over beach bag, squirrel and all.

I hoped that Chippy would reconcile herself to the basket in time, but she couldn't. The very idea of it seemed to gall her proud squirrelish insides. She gnawed endlessly at the bars and spent hours at the disheartening, monotonous, aimless, sad running back and forth that is characteristic of all caged animals. I hated to see it. I wanted to tell her not to worry, that she would soon be free. But how could I tell her? I took her out from under the basket and played with her as often as I could, but it was never enough for her. In the end she always had to go back to her awful jail.

I really looked forward to the day when I would be able to let Chippy go and I waited anxiously for the first sign that she might be ready to go off milk and start eating solid food. I even tried to hurry the process along by putting bits of lettuce and shelled sunflower seeds in front of her now and then. At first she ignored the lettuce and the seeds, but finally she began picking them up and turning them over in her paws and sniffing at them in the peculiar way squirrels have of sniffing at things—by tapping their noses against them very rapidly. But the days went by and she still didn't want anything but milk.

And while I was eager to let Chippy have her freedom, I was also a little worried about what was going to happen to her out there in the trees. Would she be okay all by herself? Would she be able to make it without me there to look after her? I remembered vaguely someone having told me once that if you come across a baby animal in the woods you should never touch it because if you do it will have the smell of human beings on it and all the other animals—even its mother—will treat it as an outcast, and I worried a lot about that. I could see Chippy—

with the smell of my hands so heavy upon her—being run out of town by the other squirrels and having to spend the rest of her life in exile somewhere far away from her real home grounds.

So I tried to get her ready for whatever lay ahead by doing all I could to make her strong and self-reliant. At least once a day we had a good long session of squirrel-in-the-tree, a game in which she was the squirrel and I was the tree and she got to run up and down and around and around on me as fast as she could go. Every day she got faster and more daring and gradually the game developed into three-squirrels-in-the-tree, a variation in which my hands became two other little squirrels that chased Chippy for a while and then turned around and let her chase them for a while.

Nothing in this life quite prepares you for the experience of playing with a squirrel—neither dogs, nor cats, nor any other animal that I know of. The idea that they can run all over you like a toy car on a track at terrific speeds and with never the slightest danger of falling off takes a good deal of getting used to, and the fact that they can run downwards, head first, and sideways either head up or head down, just as fast as they can run up and reverse their fields in the blink of an eye, also disconcerts you in the beginning. We have all witnessed, I suppose, the humiliation that usually befalls the cat that chases a squirrel up a tree. It goes sailing up the tree in fine style, quick and graceful and ferocious-looking. But of course it doesn't come anywhere near catching the squirrel for all that because the cat hasn't been born that can catch a squirrel in a tree. It stops at the first solid limb it comes to and stands there with its tail twitching, trying to look calm and collected, as if it had never really had that squirrel on its mind to start with but had just come up here actually because it had wanted to get away from things for a minute and catch a breath of fresh air and perhaps have a look around at the countryside. Then, inevitably, there comes the moment when the cat knows it can't stand around up there any longer and must try to get back down. At first it tries to come down frontwards. It doesn't seem quite right to it that it can't do it if a squirrel can, but it can't, and in the end it either inches down very awkwardly backwards, or lets go and falls, or just goes back up to the limb to wait until someone comes with a ladder.

The trouble is that a cat isn't built like a squirrel. A squirrel's back legs are hinged in such a way that they can swing around 180 degrees, just as a person can hold his arm up straight over his head and then swing it in an arc down to his side. This permits a squirrel to point its feet backwards, which is something a cat can't do, nor a dog, nor a human being, and that's all there is to it.

Only two things could make Chippy interrupt our games voluntarily—some sort of noise from outside that alarmed her or if I started walking around. In either case she would immediately run up to my shoulder to listen or to see where we were going. If I kept on walking she would stay on my shoulder and rubberneck at everything as we went from room to room. If I decided to try to kill two birds with one stone and started performing some of my humble domestic tasks while she was up there, she didn't mind that either. She liked bedmaking, desk-straightening, floor-sweeping, and she even liked dish-washing although she often got too curious for her own good about that and ran down my arm to get a closer look at what I was doing and got soapsuds on her nose for her trouble.

Six

Only five days after I had invented the laundry-basket cage another crisis arose. Chippy busted out again.

I knew that she had been spending a lot of time gnawing on the bars and that she had been shaving some of them down pretty thin, but I had still thought that the cage would last until it was time for me to let her go. Now I saw how wrong I had been. Luckily, I happened to be standing right there when she escaped. I had an appointment that I was late for and I was hurrying out of the house when I paused to look at the basket and saw Chippy's head stick through the bars.

Once again I was in the position of having to come up with a solution on the spur of the moment.

This time it was the bathroom. I picked Chippy up and put her in the bathroom and made sure that the toilet lid was down so that she couldn't possibly jump up there and fall in and put a towel in a corner for her and gave her a few sunflower seeds to play with and then closed the door behind me and left. Of course I didn't mean it to be permanent. I fully intended as soon as I came home to try to find something else that would serve as a cage. But the truth was, I didn't have all kinds of things lying around the house that could double as a cage for a squirrel. I looked around and tried to be imaginative, but in the end, as the laundry basket had just had to do before, so the bathroom finally just had to do too.

I'll say this: It was at once a good place and a bad place. It was good because Chippy thought it was okay. It had no bars, and therefore it wasn't a jail. But from my point of view it wasn't as simple as that. Think about it for a minute. A squirrel in your bathroom. It presents new complications where there are already enough complications. As long as Chippy was asleep in her towel in the corner it was fine, but when she was awake! I would open the door and there she would be, ready for play. And I was not always in the mood for play when I went into the bathroom.

But that never seemed to occur to her. Zing! She would launch herself directly at my leg. Whizz! She would be running all over me, trying to get up a game of three-squirrels-in-the-tree. It was unnerving to have something like that going on when you were trying to shave or brush your teeth, and a thousand times worse when it was something even more solemn. And this was Florida in the dead of summer, a time when people don't always go around dressed to the nines. In fact, what they usually wear is shorts and sandals and T-shirts during the waking hours and for sleeping, nothing. As a result, when Chippy launched herself at my leg what she hit more often than not was my bare calf. Then there would be that moment when I would look down and see her clinging to my leg and looking up at me with a merry glint in her eyes, completely oblivious to my agony.

The only good thing about bare legs was that she couldn't get a good enough grip on them to climb up much above the knee. So I would stand rooted to the spot after she first hit me, hoping that if I didn't do anything to encourage her she might just hang on for a minute and then drop off, as she occasionally did. But most of the time the desire for fun was too strong in her and she started trying to come the rest of the way up my leg, and if the feel of her claws sinking in while she was shinnying up as far as she could go was bad, it was nothing compared to the long slide back down.

Needless to say, stepping out of the shower was an experience. And as for those times when you felt that you had to go to the bathroom in the middle of the night— well, it was simply out of the question, unless you were prepared to do whatever you had to do in total darkness, because the minute you turned on the light you risked having Chippy think it was morning and come out of her nest wide-awake and ready for play.

Even with all the inconveniences to me of having Chippy in the bathroom, I knew that it was a much better place for her to be than cooped up under the laundry basket. And it seemed that right after she moved into the bathroom all kinds of very dramatic things began happening to her. It was like watching a flower come into bloom. Her ears gradually unfolded and stood up straight, her nose lengthened, her four little teeth grew longer, her tail bushed out handsomely and on the soles of her feet little bubbles appeared that felt like hard rubber and which obviously were meant to give her good traction when she started flying through the trees like the big squirrels.

And—perhaps most significant—she began to hide her sunflower seeds. When I gave her a few seeds each morning she set about hiding them immediately, in my slippers and under the edge of the rug and the bathmat, in corners, cracks, niches and grooves. She scampered busily all over the bathroom until every one of the seeds was hidden, and then she went back and checked on all of them several times. If for some reason known only to her a particular hiding place didn't seem quite satisfactory in retrospect, she removed the seed and found a new place for it, and then if that wasn't right she would do it again. Sometimes she would hide a single seed three or four or even five times, and even then she might look very worried about it and keep going back to sniff at it to make sure that it was still there and pull more leaves and twigs over it.

Q: What leaves and twigs?

A: That's right, there weren't any leaves and twigs in the bathroom—but she covered the seeds with them anyway. First, she found the hiding place and stuck the seed into it with her teeth. Then she pounded it in more firmly with her nose. Finally, she sat up on her haunches, leaned forward over the hiding place and stretched out her paws and pulled in the leaves and twigs to cover it. At first I didn't know what she thought she was doing. I knew the motions of course, the raking in and the patting down, because I had seen the squirrels outside doing it often enough. But this was a tiled bathroom floor! No twigs! No leaves! Couldn't she see that? Who was she trying to kid?

Finally, I realized that she wasn't trying to kid anybody. It was just centuries of *sciurus-carolinensis*-hiding-nuts-and-seeds-under-leaves-and-twigs in her blood that made her go through all those arcane gestures. And she never failed to, even when she was in a fever to get all her seeds hidden. But I must admit that now and then she could be a little perfunctory about it. Sometimes, after watching her for a while and having begun really to "see" the leaves as clearly as I think she "saw" them, I couldn't help saying, "Chip, wait a minute now, you didn't do a very good job there," when I thought she had been too casual, and sometimes she would seem to agree with me and come back to a hiding place and reach out farther and drag in more leaves to cover it better.

One thing I couldn't understand was that it never seemed to bother Chippy when in the course of cleaning the bathroom every morning I swept up all of her seeds and threw them away. I kept thinking it would make her furious, but all she ever did was hop up on my shoulder and ride around merrily while I undid her hard work of the morning before. Then when the bathroom was swept up and washed down and the rug shaken out, I would give her a fresh ration of seeds and she would go about hiding them the same as ever.

However, hiding seeds wasn't the same thing as eating them. I had begun to despair of Chippy ever going off milk when finally one morning I saw her crack open the shell of a sunflower seed. I stood there holding my breath while I watched to see if she would actually eat the seed. She kept turning it over and over in her paws and tapping her nose against it. Squirrels have four fingers on their hands—and hands is the word I might as well use from now on because that is what I think of them as and what they are actually very much like. There is, however, only a little horny stump where the thumb should be, and it is between these two stumps that they hold things they are eating or examining. I was pleased to see that Chippy knew how to hold the seed properly, but I noticed that she still couldn't sit up the way squirrels are supposed to when they're eating. If she didn't brace her back against something she would topple over. She sat in the corner with her back against the wall, sniffing and nibbling at the seed for a few minutes, and then she suddenly ran over and buried it under the rug. Well, at least it was a beginning.

Seven

Ever since she'd been living with me, Chippy had been absolutely silent. Even when she was hungry or alarmed about something she never uttered a sound. From the beginning—squirrels are such famous noisemakers out in the woods—I had been waiting for her to say something, but the days went by and she never opened her mouth. Her silence was puzzling mostly, I guess, because we're so used to cats and dogs and horses and cows and chickens and tigers and everything else never hesitating for a minute to let us know when they have something on their minds. Reticence seems as unlikely in an animal as it would be in a person.

But for all her silence, Chippy was very interested in all the sounds that came to her both from inside the house and outside. Some of them made her apprehensive, excited, occasionally almost hysterical, and some didn't. For instance, mockingbirds never seemed to bother her much, and neither did squirrels. They could sing or scold right outside her window in the bathroom and she would just listen for a minute and then go on with whatever she happened to be doing. But a blue jay's sudden sharp warning cry usually produced a violent reaction, and so did the staccato *click-click-click* of a cardinal. On windy days she was very nervous all of the time, particularly when the wind rose in gusts; but airplanes—even jets going over low—never made much of an impression on her. Perhaps the sound that she paid the most attention to was any sort of movement in the leaves outside—people walking through them, cars driving over them, cats digging in them, branches falling on them.

I tried my best to keep a catalogue in my mind of how Chippy reacted to various sounds, but it wasn't easy. For one thing, her reaction to a certain sound would be different under different conditions. If she heard a blue jay scream when she was in the midst of burying her seeds in the bathroom she would usually just freeze in her tracks and stay that way until something inside her told her that it was all right to break her pose and go back to her seeds. But if she heard the same scream while she was playing on the floor in some other room of the house she would make a wild dash for an elevated position— usually my shoulder—where she would feel safe and could keep an eye out for danger. Then she would go through a whole performance of drumming her back feet and waving her tail that might go on for really quite a long time, even though the original reason for the blue jay's warning almost always was—certainly to me and I often thought to her too—a complete mystery.

For another thing, a good part of the time I didn't even hear the sounds that excited Chippy. All of a sudden she would start acting as if she had just been handed a secret report that the entire Red Army was sneaking up on us. She would jump onto something and freeze, eyes bugging, ears straining, nostrils and tips of whiskers twitching slightly. At times like that you could pass your hand back and forth in front of her eyes and she wouldn't seem to see it, or touch her and she wouldn't seem to feel it. If I went to a window and tried to see what it was that had produced such a reaction, I might see a cat walking by, but usually I saw nothing and heard nothing, and after it was over I would just be left to try to figure out for myself what it had all been about.

Something else that puzzled me was how to interpret Chippy's more subtle reactions to sounds that disturbed her. For instance, tail-flicking. I had always thought that when squirrels flicked their tails it was intended—as I think it is with deer and rabbits—as a signal of danger to others of their own species, but after observing Chippy for a while I concluded that it really isn't any sort of signal at all but rather a form of self-expression comparable to the tail-flicking of cats. However, in the case of cats, the range of emotions expressed by tail-flicking is much broader than it is with squirrels. In cats it can mean anything from simple contentment to blue hatred, while in squirrels it always indicates displeasure—annoyance, indignation, fury. Another difference is that cats, more often than not, flick just the final third of their tails, whereas with squirrels all movements of the tail start at the base. Underneath all the plumage, a squirrel's tail is very thick at the base but quickly tapers off to nothing but a long thin string of gristle. The squirrel jerks the base of its tail and this sends ripples along the length of it. Sometimes the ripples are short and sometimes they are long, and they each mean something different. And sometimes a squirrel will wave its tail in big strokes up and down like someone waving a handker-chief, and that means something. And sometimes it swings it in great big swashbuckling circles, and that means something too. But I don't know what, and I don't think I ever will.

I also didn't understand why Chippy stood up some-times and sometimes didn't. Sometimes when she heard a noise that startled her and ran for an observation post, instead of going through the warlike drumming of the back feet or the flamboyant tail-flicking or the plain old deep freeze, she would rise up on her hind legs wherever she was and just stand there. Sometimes she stood in a sort of crouch and sometimes she stood up straight and tall, and sometimes she held both of her hands curled in on her chest and sometimes only one, and when I looked at her I would of course have not the faintest idea what it all meant. Why, for example, if she was so excited, in-stead of letting herself go and having a marvelous time shaking her tail all over the place was she just standing there so cool and dignified?

Eight

One day, as part of my program of preparing Chippy for the time when I would set her free, I took her for a walk outside. I had been wanting to do it for a couple of days but had kept talking myself out of it because of the possibility that something might go wrong, but finally I just picked her up and tucked her into the pocket of my shirt. She was still no more than four inches long, so she fitted in easily tail and all. When I went out the door I kept my hands up in a position where I could grab her if she started doing anything erratic, but she rode along quietly with nothing showing but her face, and her two hands up by her face holding onto the top of my pocket, and the tip of her tail. It was the first time she had been out under the open sky since she had come to live in my house, and I could tell that it was having a deep effect on her. In fact, I could almost hear the wheels spinning in her head as we strolled along and she looked up at the trees and the blue sky and the clouds and the birds flying overhead. I didn't overdo it. I made one loop around the property and then went back in the house. The rest of the day Chippy seemed distracted and I had a feeling that she was doing some very serious thinking about our little trip outdoors.

The next afternoon I went out to the woodpile and got an oak log about three feet long and brought it back and put it on my balcony. I arranged some cushions against the balustrade to enclose three sides of the balcony and then I went in and fetched Chippy from the bathroom. When I brought her out on the balcony I held her in my hands for a while, letting her get used to being outside again. It was a quiet afternoon. The balcony and the terrace down below were both in shade. There wasn't much wind. It seemed like an ideal time for Chippy's second experience out in the great world.

Finally, I set her down on the log. I had expected her to be nervous at first, so I wasn't surprised when she froze the instant she touched the log. I sat down on the concrete floor of the balcony—at the open end so that I would be there to field her if she suddenly took it into her head to run down the steps—and I talked to her in a soothing way to let her know that I was right there with her and she could count on me not to let any cardinals or anything else come and get her. She was flattened out on the log, lying as still as the log itself, with all four sets of claws hooked into the bark so determinedly that if I had tried to pick her up I would have had to pick up the whole log with her.

I sat there patiently and time passed. When Chippy showed no signs of relaxing even a little, I felt uneasy. I stroked her fur for a time and tickled behind her ears, and took the opportunity to try to loosen her grip on the log. But her claws wouldn't budge, and her body underneath the soft warm fur was taut and hard. I had seen her go into freezes before, but this one was positively catatonic.

And I had gone to the trouble of fencing her in with the cushions. And I had stationed myself so that I would be able to grab her if she ran down the steps. And I had thought that she was going to have such a wonderful time with her very own first log to run around on.

After about a half hour had gone by and she was still as rigid as when I had first put her down on the log, I really began to be worried. If this was how she was going to act on a pleasant afternoon just outside the door on my balcony and with me right there to look after her, what on earth was she going to do on the day when I took her across the field to one of the big oak trees and said good-bye?

"Chipper," I said, "what's the matter with you? This is your world. You're going to have to get to like it, whether you like it or not."

For a moment my words had no effect, but then a little pool of urine formed on the log behind her and trickled away down the grooves in the bark.

It looked to me like the writing on the wall.

I sat there for a few minutes more, and then to save the afternoon from being a total loss I went down and did some odd jobs around the terrace. I watered the ferns and raked some leaves and cleaned the birdbath and filled it up again with fresh water. Every once in a while I glanced up at Chippy on the balcony and saw that there was no change and just went back to fiddling around. In the meantime, life in the vicinity of the terrace went on as usual. Down on the lawn the kittens were playing in the warm grass and the full-grown cats were napping.

Lizards were frisking along the balustrades. Up above, the blue jays were watching me from the branches of the trees that overhung the terrace—an oak, a sapodilla, and a towering ficus with a trunk like a nest of colossal snakes all writhing up toward the sky—and waiting for me either to go in and bring out some bread crumbs or go away so that they could have a bath.

I had hoped that some squirrels would come by and see Chippy and let her have a look at them, but squirrels are a lot like policemen that way—when you really want one you can never seem to find any.

Finally I went back up to the balcony and sat down beside the log again. I put my hand over Chippy and was pleased to find that she wasn't quite as tense now as she had been before. I put my fingers around her middle and lifted her slightly. Then with the other hand I started prying her claws loose from the bark. It wasn't easy but in the end she let go and let me pick her up. I held her in my hands for a few minutes and felt her relax slowly. When I thought she was ready for the next step, I put her down on the floor of the balcony between me and the log. I thought that perhaps her fantastic curiosity about anything new would get the better of her now and she would want to explore the balcony so bad that she would forget about being afraid.

She flattened out and froze on the concrete at first—and I could almost see her claws trying to get a grip on it—and then she pulled her tail up over her back and started edging toward the log. Too late I saw what she had in mind. There was a hollow in the end of the log with an opening about as big around as the base of a pop bottle. Before I could cut her off, Chippy suddenly stopped edging and scooted the rest of the distance to the mouth of the hollow and disappeared into it.

When I bent down and looked up into the hollow all I

could see of my squirrel was the silver fluff of the end of her tail. I knew that it wouldn't do any good to try to coax her out, and I didn't think that I could get my fingers far enough into the hole to be able to pull her out, so I decided to wait and see if she might come out eventually by herself.

I puttered around some more down on the terrace, but nothing happened and I realized that I was going to have to do something drastic. I looked into the hollow again and still saw nothing but the tip of Chippy's tail. I held my breath and reached as far up as I could with my thumb and finger and got hold of a swatch of tail and pulled. The result astonished me. Either Chippy hadn't been able to get a good grip on the surface inside the hollow or I had taken her completely by surprise. Out she came, all in one nice easy motion.

Sadly, I took her back to the bathroom. Then I went back and got the log and brought it into the bathroom too, and in there—where she felt safe—Chippy had a fine time with it. I laid it across the open space between the toilet seat and the rim of the bathtub and that way Chippy could run around in spirals on it and cling to the underside of it and hang upside down from it by her back feet. She ran all over the log like a demon—the way she ran all over me. She had such fun with it that I didn't have the heart to take it away. So the log stayed, making the bathroom even more of a hazard than it already was.

But the fact was that every day the bathroom was becoming less and less of a good place to keep Chippy. She was beginning to want to jump. It is as much a part of a squirrel's nature to want to leap great distances as it is a bird's to fly, and there was nothing I could do about it. When I walked around the house with Chippy on my shoulder she no longer was content just to be along for the ride. She always seemed to be screwing up her nerve to jump at something, and I had to avoid getting too close to the targets that seemed to appeal to her most—the tops of cabinets, the tops of doors that were ajar, light fixtures, pictures on the wall, anything that was high up. I was afraid that she would go through a glass door or through a window, or miss what she had been aiming at altogether and plaster herself against a wall or fall to the floor and break her neck.

And the bathroom was really the worst room in the house, with all its sharp edges and hard floors and glass. When I had first put Chippy in there she had barely been able to jump onto the toilet seat. Soon she was jumping from the toilet lid to the ledge around the wash basin, where there was always a lot of trouble for her to get into. I found out very early that while she was curious about almost everything, she was most curious about the things that were none of her damn business. For example, if I indicated to her that I didn't want her messing around with the toothpaste, I could then rest assured that the toothpaste above all else would be messed around with. She loved opening containers of all kinds —boxes, cartons, tubes, vials, capsules—and she was willing to work very hard and for a long time to open something that she seemed to feel presented a special challenge to her. She was also extraordinarily good at peeling labels off things, destroying shaving brushes, and knocking just about everything in sight down onto the floor.

That was one thing, but I was afraid that while all of that was going on she was looking for new worlds to conquer too. I saw the way she kept looking up at the nearest of the towel racks—moving her head up and down and back and forth and around and around in little circles, gauging the distance, judging the angles. I knew that one of these days she was going to make that leap, and then I knew what would come after that—the other towel racks, the doorknobs, the window sill, the light fixture over the medicine cabinet, the plastic gadget up on the wall that holds the electric toothbrush that I hadn't used for about two years because the little plastic tip that you're supposed to stick the little toothbrush thing onto had gotten worn down or something and just wouldn't hold the toothbrush firmly in place anymore—on and on until, I imagined, finally—Mt. Everest!—the shower curtain rod.

Then it happened. One day I walked into the bathroom and there was Chippy looking at me from the towel rack that she had been eyeing, stretched out lengthwise, propped up on her elbows, gripping the rack with her back feet, obviously very happy. Then all the rest followed, until I finally did come in and find her up on the shower curtain rod.

That was when I knew that Chippy would have to be put into a cage. I had no choice. She was still on milk so I couldn't let her go, and I was positive that if she stayed in the bathroom any longer she would miss one of her leaps sooner or later and either kill herself outright or break a lot of bones.

Nine

I went around to some pet shops to see about buying a cage. I wanted a big one because I knew that Chippy would be terribly unhappy if she found herself confined in a small space again, but I was shocked at the prices. Big cages were expensive and I didn't want to spend a lot of money on something I would only need for a week or so. I decided that the best thing to do would be to try to knock together a cage myself.

I went to a lumber yard to buy the material for the cage and just by chance I happened to park my car in the area where they kept their rolls of fence wire. I found myself gazing at a tall coil of wire that was standing off by itself. The longer I gazed at it the more I realized it was trying to tell me something. Finally I got it. It was a perfect cage. All you would have to do was fasten it together and put something over the top. I had envisioned a traditional sort of cage that would have involved chicken wire on a wooden frame and tons of nails and screws and braces and would have taken a long time to build and probably would have turned out awful anyway. This cage would be a simple cylinder. I knew that it would be sturdy enough; the wire was very stiff, with openings one inch by two inches. I got a man to measure the piece of fence for me. It was six feet by seven feet, which meant that it would make a cage six feet tall and seven feet in circumference. I paid for it and stuck it into the back of my car and hurried home.

It took me about an hour to fasten the fence wire together so that it formed the cylinder I wanted and to find a piece of heavy screen to go over the top of the cage and secure it around the rim with clothespins. Then I stood back and looked at what I had wrought. It looked good but bare, so I went outside and searched around under the trees for some good straight branches about an inch wide and brought them back and stuck them through the cage at different angles and levels. The cage looked much better then, and I thought Chippy would have a grand time jumping from branch to branch.

I decided that the best place to put the cage was in the southeast corner of the living room because Chippy would have two windows of her own there, facing in different directions. To the south she would be able to look across the field toward the big oak trees that I thought would be her home eventually and to the east she would have the morning sun and a view of the terrace.

I tried to fix things up in the corner to make it homey for Chippy—since I had a feeling the cage was going to be a great shock to her at first, no matter how nice it was. I put down some newspaper on the floor in the corner and then went out to the woodpile and got another log and put it on the newspaper. Then I tucked a fresh towel under the log for Chippy to make a nest of and gave her a supply of sunflower seeds and lettuce. Finally, I carried the cage over to the corner and set it in place.

All that remained was for me to go and get Chippy— and I was none too soon. When I opened the bathroom door I saw that she had found her way at last into the cubbyhole where I kept the overflow from the medicine cabinet. She was happily rattling around among the bottles of mouth wash and the cans of foot powder and was about two seconds away from creating a disaster of major proportions. I hustled her out to the living room and before she had time to look the cage over and form an opinion about it and perhaps try to vote with her feet against having anything to do with it, I lifted a corner of the screen at the top and thrust her down inside. She caught onto one of the cross-branches and I pulled my hand back out of the cage and refastened the screen.

Chippy, perched on the branch, looked at me for a moment. Then she started running hysterically. I had never seen her move like that before. She went tearing around and around in the circular cage until it made me dizzy to watch her. The she went up to the screen and tried to push it open with her nose and when that didn't work went down to the bottom of the cage and started trying to gnaw the metal bars away just as she had gnawed away the plastic bars of the laundry basket. After she had gnawed for a time she seemed to realize that it wasn't going to get her anywhere, so she stopped and climbed up on one of the cross-branches and looked at me again. What could I say? I felt guilty, of course, but she had driven me to it. All of a sudden she started running around again and pushing at the screen and gnawing at the bars, but not with the same conviction, and I knew that in her heart she knew that she was trapped.

54

When she got through running she went down and examined the log. Then she sniffed the towel and punched it around a little the way she always did when she was breaking in a fresh one. Then she cracked a few sunflower seeds and nibbled at them and nibbled at her lettuce, and then she buried all of the rest of her seeds under the log and in the towel and in little holes that she dug with her claws in the newspaper. Finally, she went up and did some light acrobatics on the cross-branches and it looked as if she had begun to think that the cage wasn't really so bad after all.

It's a strange thing but the day Chippy went into the cage turned out to be the day she went off milk. At seven o'clock I gave her her bottle. She drank a few drops and then pushed the bottle away, and she never wanted it again.

Ten

So there I was.

The next morning Chippy started right in stuffing herself on sunflower seeds and lettuce, and she even ate a peanut when I tried her out on one. And she was healthy and strong and quick and there really was very little doubt in my mind that she could make it on her own on the outside now.

Yet instead of taking her out and turning her loose as I had promised myself I would the minute I thought that she was ready to go, I wavered. I was as much against having any pets as I had ever been and I honestly didn't want to keep or own or possess Chippy permanently, but still I hated to let her go. I debated the thing with myself all that day and the next, and finally I decided that I would keep her a little while longer. I didn't put myself in any corners about what I meant by "a little while," but I think that I probably meant something like a month or six weeks.

People said, "You'd better watch out. If you keep her too long you may never be able to let her go." There was a lot of truth in that, but I pretended not to hear.

Anyway, it was a whole new life for Chippy in the cage. There was always so much going on outside her windows during the day—birds flying past, kittens playing in the grass down below, squirrels running through the trees—that she had trouble keeping up with it all. And she wanted to keep up with it all. She jumped back and forth on her cross-branches, looking out of one window and then the other, listening, observing, interpreting. When the wind blew in one of her windows it fascinated her. She would stand up on her hind legs on one of the branches, hold onto the bars with her hands and stick her nose out eagerly, smelling the wind as if it were bringing her a stream of important messages.

And it was a new life for me too. It was much easier on my nerves to have Chippy in a place where I didn't have to worry constantly about something happening to her. Of course I felt guilty at the same time. I don't like cages. I can't stand to see animals shut up in them. And here I had put Chippy into one. I kept watching her for the first couple of days to see if she hated the cage, telling myself that if it looked as if she did I would turn her loose immediately. But except for that time at the very beginning she never showed any signs that she hated it. I think this was because the cage was so big that she never felt trapped in it, as I'm sure she had in the laundry basket.

She settled into a regular routine very quickly. She woke up long before I did in the morning and started running at full speed. She would run up one side of the cage to the top, then upside down across the underside of the screen, down the other side, across the floor, up the first side to the top again, over and over. She would run for half an hour and sometimes even an hour without a pause and the amazing thing was that it never seemed to tire her. She never panted, her sides never heaved, her tongue never hung out. When she did stop running it always looked as if she had stopped only because she had gotten bored with it.

When I got up Chippy was usually still on her rounds. I would sit at the table in the living room and have a cup of coffee. Chippy wouldn't pay any attention to me, and I wouldn't do anything to disturb her. I knew that the running was very serious business, like the hiding of the sunflower seeds.

After the running came the grooming, which was also pretty serious. Squirrels are always washing, but they have no saliva to do it with in their mouths. Instead, they use moisture from their noses.

Chippy gave herself two or three good stiff wash-ups a day and quick lick-and-a-promise jobs throughout the day. When she was getting ready to wash you could always tell because she would suddenly drop everything and go and sit up somewhere very still for a moment with a sort of far away look in her eye. If you knew what was coming it was rather like watching someone trying to bring on a sneeze, which, actually, was just what it was. Finally she would bring her thumbs up to her nose, squeeze her eyes shut and let out a series of little sneezes. Each time she sneezed she closed up one nostril with one of her thumbs and wet the other thumb with the spray that came out of the open nostril. She kept on sneezing that way, rocking her head slightly from side to side as she did it, until both of her thumbs were wet. Then she started washing. She usually began with her ears and her face and went about it much the way a cat does. She put her thumbs back behind her ears and brought them forward over her ears and down her face to her nose. At the end of each stroke she sneezed a little more moisture onto her thumbs, and when she finished the short fur along the bridge of her nose would be left standing up, making her look for a moment rather like a little gray lamb.

After cleaning her face, she washed her forearms and the backs of her hands. For this she used her nose, rubbing it over the fur and sneezing as she moved along. Then she combed out the hair with her two long lower teeth. She did her sides and chest and stomach and hind legs and feet the same way, and if she wanted to concentrate on a foot she simply would grab hold of it with both hands and pull it up to her nose so that she could work on it more easily. When she began grooming, her movements were always slow and dreamy, but as she went on with it the tempo gradually picked up and her nose flew faster and faster.

Last on the agenda was always her tail. When she had taken care of everything else she reached around behind her and took hold of it firmly with both hands and brought it up to her nose. Then she went to work on it with a great deal of snuffling and sneezing, washing and combing it carefully from the base out to the tip.

When the running and the grooming were finally over with I cleaned Chippy's cage. One of its advantages was that it was easy to clean. Since it had no bottom, all I had to do was lift it, squirrel and all, out of the corner, bundle up the used newspapers and lay down fresh ones, and put the cage back, and that was that. In this connection I should say here that I was charmed, as I got to know Chippy, to learn that squirrels are gratifyingly—even astonishingly—subtle in the matter of their excreta. For instance, a baby squirrel's droppings are no more than flyspecks, and as the squirrel gets older all that happens is that the flyspecks get a little bigger and more numerous. They have no odor to speak of and—considering what one is usually confronted with in this line from pets—are altogether inoffensive.

When I got through cleaning the cage I gave Chippy a fresh supply of sunflower seeds and lettuce. She went right to work hiding the seeds and just as frantically as she had every morning in the bathroom. In fact, it seemed to me that after she stopped taking milk there was a daily increasing urgency to the way she fussed over her seeds. She scurried around even faster looking for places to bury them and spent even more time digging them up and burying them again.

I began to worry about her diet because I thought she needed more than sunflower seeds and lettuce. I gave her peanuts now and then but she didn't like them much. If I gave them to her in the shell she just buried them right away, and if I gave them to her out of the shell she would turn them over in her hands and sniff them and gnaw on them a little and then bury them. I kept asking people for advice about what to feed her but nobody seemed to know. Even veterinarians and pet shop owners didn't know. Few of them had ever had anything to do with squirrels. They knew that they were herbivorous and that was about the extent of it. "Give him bread," one man told me. "They're crazy about bread, believe me." But Chippy wouldn't touch it. "They go for all kinds of fruit," someone else said. But Chippy didn't want anything but perhaps a bit of banana now and then. "Listen, they're just like canaries," another man said. "Give him the same sort of stuff you'd give a canary." So I bought a whole bunch of canary stuff and took it home and Chippy was fascinated by all the jars and the brightly colored boxes, but she ignored the stuff in them.

"Peanuts," everybody said. "Squirrels love peanuts."

"Not my squirrel," I said.

"Well, you just give him a pecan sometime if you want to see some action," they said. "Or a nice juicy walnut, or a chestnut, or an almond, or a cashew. Squirrels love nuts. Everybody knows that. It's just like bears and honey."

The trouble was that I couldn't find any pecans, or walnuts, or chestnuts, or almonds, or cashews around anywhere. Not fresh ones, at any rate. Of course there were lots of salted nuts available in cans and in little cellophane packages, but I covered the produce departments of most of the grocery stores for miles around and the closest I came to finding fresh nuts in the shell was some almonds at a roadside stand out in the country. Even then it turned out they were from the crop of the year before and had been frozen over the winter and were tasteless.

Everyone said, "You'll have to wait until October."

So I waited, but in the meantime I kept a close watch on the squirrels outside. If I saw one chewing on a leaf or twig I would get hold of one like it and take it to Chippy. She was always very interested in anything that I brought her from outdoors, even pebbles and little lumps of dirt. In fact, she was so captivated by dirt that I had to keep potted plants out of her reach or she would climb right into the pot and start burrowing in the dirt, snuffling and sneezing, finding things that were absolutely invisible to me and eating them with great enthusiasm.

I knew that squirrels liked coconuts. They can't open mature coconuts but they can open young ones—before the crown of the husk turns fibrous and the inner shell gets hard as cast iron. They eat the crisp white meat and drink the coconut water. Since coconut palms produce coconuts all year around, squirrels that live in them always have a good supply of food and drink near at hand, which can be a comfort in an emergency. For instance, during long dry spells you will always see green coconuts with their tops chewed away scattered around the bases of palms in which squirrels are living. The squirrels have cut their stems and dropped them and opened them on the ground, for their water. I brought Chippy the very young coconuts—about the size of golfballs—that fall whenever a strong wind blows. She liked to gnaw on them, even though there was really nothing on the inside of them once she got there. She liked ferns and flowers too, particularly the tender curled tips of new ferns and the nectar that she found in the base of the hibiscus.

Eleven

Once I was convinced that Chippy didn't hate the cage,
the next thing I wanted to do was make a house for her.
Somehow it didn't seem quite right for her to go on sleeping in a towel on the floor now that she was getting to be
a grown-up squirrel. Of course the question that arose
immediately was, what would she think of the idea? I
could see myself going to a lot of trouble making a very
nice house for her and then having her ignore it completely.

But I settled down one night with pencil and paper and
set to work designing a house that I thought would be
suitable for a squirrel. First I drew a plain box with an
open end. That was the basic plan of the house. Then I
added on a porch by extending the bottom piece of the
box a little and put in four windows—and the house

was ready to go from the designing to the building stage. I had some heavy-gauge illustration board on hand that I thought would be good material to make the house out of, and after a certain amount of heavy breathing over measurements and some tense moments with a frighteningly sharp mat knife, I succeeded in cutting out the necessary parts for the world's first prefab squirrel house.

Next I painted green shutters on the windows, and after that I assembled the house, using strips of masking tape to hold it together. Then I cut up one of Chippy's old towels and stuffed some pieces of it into the house to make it a little cosier. When it was all finished the house didn't look bad and I thought it would be sturdy enough.

My plan was to run a branch across the cage up near the top and hang the house from it. I punched some holes in the roof of the house and laced short lengths of twine through them. Then I took a chair over to the cage and climbed up on it and started taking the screen off the top of the cage as quietly as possible. I hoped I would be able to install the house without waking Chippy up, but I had barely gotten started when there was movement in the towel under the log down below. The face of a squirrel whose repose has been interrupted at an ungodly hour of the night appeared. I tried to convey to her the idea that everything was perfectly all right, that I really wasn't doing anything much and that I would be through with it very soon anyway, but I could have saved my breath.

Chippy came out of the towel the rest of the way, stretched and yawned, and then climbed up on her log to get a better look at me. She stayed there for a moment, obviously hoping that now that she had caught me at whatever it was that I was up to, I would have the decency to knock it off and turn out the lights and go to bed.

I was trying to stick a branch through the top of the cage at the time and was having a little trouble getting it to go through the opening between the bars because it was too thick. I was twisting it around and around trying to force it through and skinning off a lot of bark in the process which was raining down on the floor of the cage. And I was jiggling the cage and in general making quite a fuss, and finally Chippy saw that she would have to come up and see what was going on.

She climbed up the side of the cage nearest me and when she reached the top she hopped over onto my arm. Then she went down my arm to where my fingers were holding onto the branch and checked out the branch to see that it wasn't dangerous to squirrels by sniffing it over and gnawing it a little. When she saw that it was harmless she ran back and forth along it several times and hung from it by her back feet, while I tried to hold it steady. Finally, she ran back up my arm and over my shoulder and down the back of my shirt and pants to the seat of the chair I was standing on, dropped to the floor and went off exploring.

I didn't like the idea of her running loose when I couldn't keep an eye on her, but I decided that in the present circumstances the best course was to let her be and get on with the job of installing the house. After I managed to slide the branch all the way through the cage I got the house from the table in the kitchen where I had left it. I took a quick look around for Chippy at the same time but didn't see her anywhere, which was ominous. I worked as fast as I could fastening the house underneath the branch with the pieces of twine that I had laced through the holes in the roof, but I kept bungling the tying of the knots and bobbling the house around. One time the house slipped out of my hands completely and fell to the floor, and I had to climb down from my chair and lift up the side of the cage to retrieve it. All the while I wondered what sort of trouble Chippy was into, half expecting to hear a loud crash from somewhere at any moment.

When I had succeeded at last in attaching the house securely to the branch it occurred to me for the first time that there really was no way for Chippy to get into the house—if she should ever actually want to—except by climbing down from the branch above. That was making it too difficult. So I put in another branch, this one running across the cage just a couple of inches below the house so that Chippy would be able to step from the branch right up onto her front porch.

Then, nervously, I went on a Chippy hunt. I found her just in the nick of time in the pantry shinnying up a broom handle toward a shelf where there were any number of bottles and cans of floor polish and drain cleaner waiting for her to shovel them overboard.

I gave Chippy a lot of sweet talk on the way back to the cage, trying to put her in the right frame of mind for what was waiting for her there. It didn't do much good. When she got a load of the house she sprang out of my hands and clung to my shoulder, looking as if she had seen a twenty-foot boa constrictor in her cage rather than a little cardboard house with four windows, a porch and green shutters. Then she leaped over to the cage and started moving cautiously around the rim, fixing the house first with one eye and then the other. She kept her tail pulled around to the side so that it was a shield between her and the house, and her whiskers twitched feverishly as she sniffed the air.

Well, of course, I hadn't expected immediate acceptance. So I wasn't too disappointed at her reaction. It looked as if I really had my work cut out for me though, trying to convince her that it would be much more dignified and properly squirrelish for her to sleep up there in the house instead of down on the floor in a towel. I envisioned a long slow process in which she would gradually get used to the house being in her cage to start with, followed by a program in which I would put some of her sunflower seeds in the house each day, hoping that she would go in after them and in that way get used to being in the house, followed, perhaps, finally, by a decision on her part actually to move in.

In the meantime I knew my duty. I stood up on the chair right behind her, letting her know that I was with her all the way and that if the house got out of hand I would jump right in and help her teach it a lesson it wouldn't forget in a thousand years.

After a thorough reconnaissance of the position, Chippy began closing in on the house. First she went gingerly out on the upper branch to look down at it, then she went out on the lower branch to look up at it. She edged out on the lower branch until she was close enough to sniff the porch. Then she bit it. Once she had done that and knew that the house wasn't alive, she grew very bold. She hopped up on the porch and stuck her head into the house. Then she was halfway in. Then she was all the way in. Then things began happening. There was a great commotion in the house—much snuffling and knocking against the walls and the ceiling. From where I was standing I couldn't see into the doorway and I was afraid to move because I thought that if I made any noise Chippy might panic and feel trapped in the house and come hurtling out of it and never want to go back in again. But through the windows I could see gray fur and the swishing of her tail and I got an occasional glimpse of one of her big shiny eyes. She was turning around and around in circles and seemed to be rearranging the pieces of towel that I had stuffed into the house by pulling up folds of the cloth with her teeth and patting them down again with her hands.

This continued for several minutes. Then all of a sudden there was silence. I got down from my chair and went around to the other side of the cage to look into the doorway of the house. I saw that Chippy with all of her going around in circles and pulling up and patting down had made a nice little hollow for herself in the towel. She was lying on her side with her tail over her face, sound asleep.

Twelve

That was how things always ended. Very abruptly. Just as Chippy had turned her back on her bottle one day and never had wanted milk again after that, so after she moved into her house that night she never slept on the floor again one single time.

I think that one of the things Chippy liked most about her house was that I had hung it up near the very top of the cage. Since I'm less than six feet tall and the cage was six feet even, this meant that when she was in her house she was above me, which I'm sure she considered the truly correct, appropriate and natural spatial relationship of squirrel to man. She liked to look down on me from up there. I would glance up at odd moments and see one of those marvelous unblinking eyes watching me through a window or from the doorway.

Another thing I knew that she must have liked was that I had faced the house toward the east window so that the prevailing wind would flow through the door and out the windows. August is a brutal month in this part of Florida. It isn't just that the heat is so ferocious during the day but that at night it's not any better, and any cooling off that occurs between, say, four o'clock in the morning and dawn is made up for as soon as the sun has been in the sky for thirty minutes. Now at least Chippy had the wind, which of course had never touched her down on the floor. Besides that, in the house she could sleep without any covering over her. It seemed that she couldn't sleep unless she felt enclosed and protected and hidden, and that was why even on the hottest nights on the floor she had insisted in wrapping herself up in a towel. Now, apparently, the house gave her the feeling of security that she needed and while she slept in the hollow she had made in the pieces of towel in the house, she never pulled anything over her.

And at last she had a place to hide some of her seeds where they would be safe from me when I cleaned up her cage. She still buried most of her seeds in the newspaper on the floor when I gave them to her in the morning, but now she also took a few of them up to her house each time and hid them in the corners and under the bedding. She kept other things up there too—pebbles and baby coconuts, pieces of bark, peanuts, twigs. And the more her treasures accumulated the more time she spent fussing over them. It seemed that she had to interrupt whatever she was doing a hundred times a day to run up to her house to check that everything was still all there. There was no end to the arranging and rearranging and the covering over with leaves and patting down that all of this constant checking required, and just when you would swear that everything must finally have been taken care of, the whole process would start over again. I would even hear her at night after the lights had been turned out and good nights had been said and we were both supposed to have been asleep—out there in her house counting her money.

Then one day there was something new. Chippy began tearing strips of newspaper from the bottom of her cage and taking them up to her house. She did it with an intensity that was alarming to see. It would go on for a few minutes and then stop, and then a little later she would be at it again—running up and down her cage like a little elevator with strips of newspaper in her mouth. I hadn't a notion of what she was trying to prove stuffing her house with paper like that, but that evening a strong wind came up and for the first time in a long while I heard thunder in the distance. When the storm began later on and I went to close the window next to Chippy's cage and looked up at her house to see if she was all right, there simply was nothing of her to be seen. She had completely blocked up the doorway and all of the windows with the strips of newspaper and to look at the house you never would have guessed that there was a squirrel inside.

After that I always knew when bad weather was coming well in advance because Chippy always barricaded her house the same way. The only difference was that as she got older she switched from using plain newspaper to a combination of newspaper and twigs from the oak branches I put into her cage every few days. She would nip off a twig and hold it in her hands and move it back and forth in her mouth like a gigantic harmonica testing the balance of it until she found the middle of it. Then she clamped it between her teeth and charged through the door of her house full speed. This would bend the twig in the middle and make the two leafy ends fold back behind her as she sailed on through to the rear wall of the house, and as she kept on bringing in more twigs a tightly thatched nest would begin to form around her until finally there would just be a very small space for her to curl up in at the center and a little opening to go in and out of. When she went into her house for the last time she would close up the opening with newspaper, and that would be the last I would see of her until the storm had passed.

In between storms, Chippy pulled her nests apart and threw out the newspaper and twigs because she liked to have the wind blowing through her house, but when September came and it started raining almost continuously because of the hurricanes forming off the coast, she had to keep her house closed up all the time.

Yet, strangely, when a hurricane actually passed through our neighborhood in late September, Chippy wouldn't go into her house the whole time. As the storm came closer I waited for the moment when she would run up to her house and disappear for the duration, but all she did was run around nervously in her cage or lie on a branch listening to the rising wind.

In the afternoon I went through the usual motions of getting ready for a hurricane—boarding up windows and putting the garbage cans in the tool shed and all the rest of it. Then just before dark I took a walk down toward the bay. Even though the wind was blowing hard already, it was quiet and still among the big trees on the high ground, but when I started down the slope and came out from under the trees I felt the wind in my face. It was warm and sticky and smelled of brine. The sky was low with the clouds sailing by very fast. The tide was high, which was bad. I knew that in a few hours, in the blackness, the wind would start driving the bay across the sea wall and we would have breakers on our front lawns.

When I got back to the house it was dark inside. I really expected to find that Chippy had gone to her house, but when I turned on the lights I saw her lying on a branch just as I had left her. I had supper and attended to the final preparations for the storm. I filled the bathtub with water, made sure that a couple of windows on the leeward side of the house were open and put candles and matches in all of the rooms. Then I listened to the weather reports until the lights flickered and went out for the last time around eleven.

By that time the wind was roaring in the tops of the trees and unknown things were beginning to thud against the house. The only sensible thing to do then was to go to bed and try to sleep through the rest of it. But I couldn't sleep. I lay in bed with my eyes wide open thinking of all the things I should have done that I hadn't done. I hadn't boarded up enough of the windows. I hadn't found a really safe place for my car. And as if the howling wind and the lashing rain weren't enough, a continual pounding of thunder shook the house and a flashing of lightning lighted up the rooms with ghastly white light in a way that made me keep wishing I had been a much nicer person in my life.

I got up many times in the night to prowl through the house and reassure myself that pieces of it weren't coming loose and blowing away. Every time I went near Chippy's cage I saw her in the lightning flashes there on her branch.

I fell asleep toward dawn and slept until ten. By then the storm had passed and was in the process of blowing itself out up around Lake Okeechobee. The sun was shining between rain squalls and it shone much brighter through my windows than it usually did at that time of the morning because the trees were so bare. I looked for Chippy first thing. She was sound asleep in her house.

Thirteen

One night—not long after the hurricane—something woke me up. I lay in bed listening. I had no idea what had awakened me, but I had a definite feeling that something was wrong. After a while I got up and went to the living room. I didn't turn on any lights but just stood in the doorway listening. At first I didn't hear anything. Then I heard a faint sound from the direction of Chippy's cage and I turned on a light and saw her crouching on the floor at the bottom of her cage. It surprised me because I knew that she didn't like to come out of her house late at night.

I started over to the cage to have a look at her, but just then she ran up to her house and disappeared inside.

A couple of nights later more or less the same thing happened all over again. This time I had stayed up late working and when I finally went to bed I couldn't go to sleep right away. As I lay there I heard a sound from the living room. It wasn't a very loud sound and at first I thought I would ignore it, but then I remembered my recent experience with Chippy and decided that I had better go and check on her.

When I turned on the light in the living room I saw that she was down on the floor again. She didn't move when I went over to her and it seemed to me that she looked stunned. But when I put my fingers through the bars and wiggled them at her she came over to them the way she always did. And she let me rub her nose as well as I could through the bars with my finger. After that she went back up to her house, and I was left to wonder whether or not there was anything to worry about in all of this. Both this time and the other time Chippy may have come out of her house for some reason and gotten confused in the darkness and fallen, and if that was the case then obviously there was something to worry about. But I wasn't sure that she had fallen either time and if she had simply begun wanting to fiddle around on the floor in the middle of the night I couldn't see that it was anything to worry about.

I think I convinced myself in the end that I didn't have to worry because it just didn't seem possible that Chippy, who could stick like glue to almost anything, would fall, even in the dark. Two days later I found out how wrong I was.

I was working at the table in the living room. It was around three o'clock in the afternoon and Chippy was taking a nap in her house and everything was peaceful. Then I heard a slight scraping noise and from the corner of my eye I saw the front end of Chippy's house tip downward a little and her slide out of it. She fell onto the log at the bottom of her cage and then tumbled down to the floor and lay there on her side with her eyes closed. I lifted the cage away and started to pick her up, but then I thought that it might be best to let her lie there for a minute. I hoped that she had only had the wind knocked out of her, but when several minutes had gone by and she didn't move at all I began to be afraid that she was really hurt.

I felt very helpless and the longer she lay there the worse the feeling got. Aside from everything else, it was terribly sad to see her lying on her side out in the open when that was something she would never have done voluntarily. I kept starting to pick her up and then thinking that it would probably be better not to. In fact, I finally put the cage back in place so that if she opened her eyes she would feel enclosed and secure and in familiar surroundings.

I got up on my chair and took the screen off the top of the cage. Then I understood everything. Some of the knots in the twine holding the house to the branch above it had worked loose and when Chippy in her sleep had rolled over and moved her weight to the front end of the house it had tilted downward and she had slid right out. The scraping sound I had heard had been her claws try-ing to get a grip on the slick surface of the illustration board. I was sure that it had been the same all three times. I tied the knots again and tried to do a better job this time, but I felt terrible for not having foreseen what could happen.

There was nothing to do but wait. Finally about an hour after she had fallen Chippy opened her eyes and dragged herself to the log and crawled up on it, and for the rest of the afternoon she crouched there motionless. As the sun was setting, she stirred again. When the sun was low like that it filled the room with the shadows of the trees dancing in the wind and it could fool you.

Things seemed to be moving that weren't and the sun kept blinding you as it found holes in the foliage to shoot you straight in the eyes. I was sitting in a chair watching Chippy and a couple of times I thought I saw her move, but when I looked again I realized that it was only an illusion. Finally, as the light faded, she came down off the log and hobbled over to the side of the cage and started climbing slowly up to her house.

It took her a long time to reach her house. When she made it at last and went inside, I looked in her window and saw her turning around and around as if she were trying to find a comfortable way to lie down and couldn't. In the end she just crouched in a corner and let her head droop down in a way that worried me because I had never seen her do it before. I was positive that the other two times she had fallen she had probably been able to twist herself around in the air and land on her feet but that this time she had landed on her head.

I reached into her house and rubbed her nose for a bit and felt her over to see if anything was broken or there were any bumps. I couldn't find anything. I had hung a little water bowl in her cage of the type that you put in bird cages and I brought it over and put it on her porch to see if she wanted any. She wouldn't even look at it, so I put a drop on my finger and held it under her nose. She still wasn't interested. I got her some cold fresh lettuce from the icebox but she wouldn't take that either. I cracked open a couple of sunflower seeds but she didn't want them. I tried her on ferns and leaves and flowers and anything else that she had ever shown the slightest liking for in the past, but she refused everything except a bit of cold honeydew melon, and when she ate that it didn't make me feel any better because she let me hold it for her while she nibbled at it rather than taking it in her own hands as she normally would have done.

After she ate the melon she went to sleep. I went out later and when I came back she was still in the same position. I thought of waking her up to see if she would eat something else or drink some water, but I decided against it and went to bed hoping that she would be much better in the morning.

But she wasn't any better in the morning. It was strange to go into the living room and look at her cage and not see her on her morning rounds. She was crouching in her house with her head drooping and didn't even stir when I spoke to her. I sat at the table staring at the cage and drinking one cup of coffee after another and feeling worse and worse. Finally, because I couldn't bear any longer not doing anything, I started calling veterinarians. I had been pretty sure that it would be a losing game and I was disappointed to be proven right. I would tell them that my little squirrel had fallen on her head and looked bad and I was worried about her and they would tell me that they were sorry but they didn't know anything about squirrels because squirrels were wild animals and wild animals were an entirely different matter from dogs and cats, which was what they knew something about.

My pessimism intensified. I got up on a chair and removed Chippy's house from the branch and carried her in it into the bedroom and put it down on the bed. The bright morning sunshine fell across the bed and it reminded me of that first morning, when I had brought Chippy up out of the beach bag and put her on the bed in the sunshine. She had been full of life then but now she just crouched in her house, and looking at her I felt I had made a terrible mistake in deciding to keep her instead of letting her go. Everything had been all right until I had let my sentimentality and my selfishness get the better of me. And now because of that Chippy would never play in the leaves out in the woods, would never chase around the trunks of the big oaks and fling herself through the high branches or stretch out on her stomach on a limb in the heat of the day and feel the cool wind from the bay in her face.

I reached into the box and took hold of Chippy as gently as I could and brought her out. She crouched on the bed, looking very beautiful, but with her head down just the way it had been in the house.

On an impulse, I called the zoo in a nearby city. It was an act of desperation and I know that I must have sounded pretty desperate to the woman who answered the telephone.

"I want the lion doctor," I said.

"The who?" she said.

"I can't remember his name," I said, "but there was a story about him in the paper the other day. It said that he has a miraculous way with wild animals and kept calling him the lion doctor."

"You must mean Dr. Harrison," the woman said.

"That sounds right."

"You want to speak to him?"

"Yes."

"Would you mind telling me why you want to speak to him?"

"Because I need help," I said. "I'm at the end of my rope."

I told the woman about Chippy and she seemed very sympathetic and said that she would try to put me through. After a lot of clicking the lion doctor himself was there on the telephone speaking to me.

"Yes?" he said.

I told him about Chippy and he too sounded very sympathetic. In fact, he didn't seem to mind at all that I had called him up to tell him about my squirrel.

"I'm afraid we have to face the fact that there probably has been some brain damage," he said. "It sounds like it, but it's impossible for me to tell how serious it is without seeing her. Anyway, she's young and if it isn't too serious she'll get over it and be as good as new in a few days. On the other hand, if it is serious, that's another matter. There are certain things you should be watching for. First—"

"Wait a minute," I said. "Something's happening."

I had been watching Chippy while I talked and suddenly her eyes, which until then had been black and shiny as always, had clouded over. It was a frightening and depressing thing to see.

"Her eyes have turned white," I said. "It looks as if a film has come over them."

"Then there's definitely been some brain damage," the doctor said.

"Is this very bad?" I asked.

"Not necessarily."

"Is she going to die now?"

"I don't know," the doctor said.

"You can tell me," I said.

"All I can tell you is that I don't think you should give up hope so easily," the doctor said.

He told me to watch Chippy closely in the next couple of days and call him again if she didn't improve. The most important thing to keep an eye on, he said, was the way she moved. If she displayed a tendency always to want to go in circles, then the outlook would be quite grim.

Right after I hung up Chippy blinked her eyes and the white film disappeared completely. Then she ate some lettuce when I offered it to her and even sat up and held it properly in her hands. After that she started running around on the bed as if nothing had ever happened. It seemed as if all the effects of her fall had vanished at the same moment that the film had vanished from her eyes. She held her head up in her normal way and when she moved she didn't show any tendency at all to go in circles.

Later on I put Chippy's house back in the cage, but this time I made sure to put a strip of cardboard across the bottom of the doorway so that she would have something to cling to if she started falling out.

Miraculously all was well again. But I had learned a few lessons from the experience. The most crucial one was that I had better be careful of Chippy's health because in an emergency there was no one to turn to, except, perhaps, the lion doctor.

PART TWO

Fourteen

I think this has been a fairly pleasant story so far. In our first three months together Chippy and I had some bad moments and survived them and had a lot of good moments too, and you would have thought—wouldn't you? —that through it all our understanding and trust of each other would have been growing steadily and we would have been becoming faster friends.

Well, that was what I thought was happening too. But I was wrong. I was wrong about everything. The fact was that I had many hard truths to learn about Chippy in particular and squirrels in general and while I was learning them our story stopped being so pleasant and I had to live through some experiences that were very painful to me, both physically and spiritually.

The hardest truth was that Chippy was not tame even

though I had saved her from a cat and raised her on a bottle and she lived in my house with me and let me hold her in my hands sometimes. She was wild and the wildness of squirrels is an awesome wildness.

I began to understand this one morning in early October when I was sitting at the table in the kitchen reading the paper and minding my own business. Chippy was playing on the window sill. Suddenly I became aware of a presence and I lowered my paper a little and saw that she had hopped over onto the table and was advancing silently and cautiously on a piece of French bread that had caught her eye. She wasn't too crazy about bread of any kind, but she liked French bread a little when I gave it to her and quite a lot when she stole it. I didn't mind her stealing the bread but I didn't want her walking around on the kitchen table and lately I had begun a campaign to try to keep her from it.

"No squirrels on the kitchen table," I said, and fluttered my paper at her.

I spoke softly and fluttered the paper at her softly. That was usually enough to send her dashing away, but this time she ignored me and kept on sneaking up on the piece of bread. I fluttered the paper again, but still softly, and she retreated to the window sill. I went back to my reading but a few minutes later I looked over the paper and saw her creeping up on the piece of bread again, this time from a slightly different angle.

"No squirrels on the kitchen table," I said, and fluttered my paper again, this time not so softly.

I knew Chippy was very sensitive to the sounds that you can make with paper. I think she related it to the rustling of leaves. Once, without thinking, I had balled up a piece of paper almost under her nose and I had never forgotten her reaction. I had been working at the table in the living room and she had been sitting on the table near my typewriter, grooming herself. I had gotten disgusted with something I had written and had suddenly crumpled up the piece of paper that I'd been writing on. Chippy had risen straight up about a foot and a half, twisting herself violently around in midair. When she had come down she had fallen against my typewriter, which had scared her even more. She had leaped into the air again but this time had missed the table coming down and had landed with a thump on the floor. Then she had run back to her cage and had hurtled around inside it for a long time, looking thoroughly terrified.

The last fluttering of the newspaper frightened Chippy. She jumped away from me and then lost her footing on the slick formica of the tabletop and skittered around frantically like an ice-skater trying to keep himself from falling. Finally she fell to the floor. I reached down to pick her up but she ran away from me. She climbed up on a chair and jumped over to the window sill and then started coming back toward the table.

When I saw her coming it gave me a funny feeling because I had a premonition that this time she wasn't coming for the bread but for me. I sat still, hoping I was wrong. She hopped onto the table and advanced on me swiftly. She feinted once to the right and then launched herself at me. I held up my left hand to protect myself and she hit my hand with all fours and clung there just long enough to give me a quick deep bite on my thumb. Then she leaped across the front of me to my right forearm and from there to my left leg and finally down to the floor.

The whole thing only took a moment but when it was over I had a bloody thumb and long gashes from her back claws on my right arm and left leg. I sat there dumbfounded, looking at myself. Getting scratched by Chippy was nothing new, but this was the first time she had ever hurt me deliberately.

I went to the bathroom and washed the blood off and

when I came out I found Chippy running around happily in the living room. She had made use of the time I had spent in the bathroom to go on an expedition to the pantry and she had found the big bag of sunflower seeds that I kept in there. She was having a grand time bringing in seeds one by one in her teeth and hiding them in the rug. It was an oriental rug and she only hid the seeds in the dark places in the pattern. I guess she thought everything else was flat but that the dark places must be crevices. She parted the nap of the rug with her claws and stuffed in a seed and then covered it over with imaginary leaves.

I sat down and watched, feeling bewildered and depressed. It all seemed so wrong. Here I was all cut up and hurting like hell and there she was running around acting as if nothing had happened. What I wanted to do was grab her and give her a damn good scolding followed by a damn good spanking. But I knew that she probably wouldn't have tolerated a scolding and certainly not a spanking.

As I watched, Chippy ran out to the pantry and came back a moment later with another seed. She started to look around for a place in the rug to hide it and then abruptly changed her mind and came dashing straight toward me. My heart stopped cold when I saw her coming, but all she wanted to do was hide the seed somewhere on my person. She jumped up on my shoulder and stood on her hind legs to consider my hair as a hiding place, parting it here and there and trying to get the seed to go in and stay in. When that didn't work she looked my right ear over, sticking her nose in it and behind it and making the low murmuring sound that she always made when she was supremely happy. Finally she pulled my collar out and stuck the seed down it while I died, as usual, from the feel of those whiskers against the back of my neck.

She ran away then, but was back a minute later to check on the seed, pulling it out of my collar and turning it over and over in her hands while she tapped at it with her nose to make sure that it was still intact. She hid it again, scurried away, disappeared under the couch, came shooting out, disappeared again, popped up out of nowhere to give my big toe a playful nip, tore up one side of an armchair and down the other, hopped onto my shoulder again, pulled out her seed and this time decided to eat it.

She sat on my shoulder with her back toward me and her big tail brushing my left ear and cracked open the seed and ate it. Then in one shot she leaped over onto my right knee and sat up and began giving herself a quick grooming.

After that she ran out to the kitchen and I looked through the doorway and saw her climb up on the chair on which I had been sitting before and from there jump up onto the kitchen table. I saw her snatch up the piece of French bread, but to make sure that I saw that she finally had it she came over to the edge of the table with it sticking out in front of her like an enormous cigar and stood there a minute in my full view. Then she streaked away to the window sill. I heard her climb up the screen, hop onto the curtain rod, walk along the rod and jump over onto the tall wooden cabinet that stood in the corner.

I went on into the kitchen and sat down at the kitchen table again. From the corner of my eye I could see Chippy up on top of the cabinet, and I could hear her gnawing away at the bread. I knew her eyes were on me and I knew what she was thinking—that I had definitely gotten out of line for a minute there and unfortunately she had had to step on me a little but that we were right back to normal now and everything was perfectly fine with us again.

Fifteen

I sat at the kitchen table that morning for quite a while, thinking about the way Chippy had attacked me and the meaning of it, and that led me inevitably to some serious thinking about the exact nature of our relationship.

You couldn't really have said that we were master and pet. A pet, ideally, is an animal that freely and openly recognizes someone as its master—lives by his rules, respects his power, admits his superiority in all things, and worships the ground he walks on.

With Chippy and me it wasn't like that. In fact, as she matured her whole life style seemed increasingly an assertion of her joyous spirit of independence. It was disturbing. A pet is supposed to come when it's called, cringe when it's scolded, and do tricks for its supper. Chippy never came when I called her unless she happened to be headed in that direction anyway, ignored me when I tried to scold her, and wouldn't have known what a trick was if one had walked up in broad daylight and kicked her in the pants.

The truth was that a side of me really wanted her to be a pet. It was the side of me that liked things to add up, that wanted all relationships to be clear-cut, that felt strongly that biting someone is never a permissible way of settling a difference of opinion. Well—to go all the way, to pour my heart out, to be absolutely embarrassing about it—I guess I wished that Chippy would curl up in my lap and go to sleep sometimes, roll over when I asked her to, bring me my slippers, play dead, act a little grateful now and then, let me feel that I was boss.

I think I even wished occasionally that I could take her out and show her off to my friends. None of them had ever seen her because it was generally understood among them at that time that I was working very hard on a book and didn't want any visitors. But I talked about her often when I went out and they were curious and asked if I wouldn't bring her by one day so that they could see her. I always said I would, but it was impossible. I was afraid even to step out the door with her on my shoulder because I thought she might have a nervous breakdown at the first strange sound she heard or try to run away from me or something, much less take her on tour. I could have done it only if I had put her in a cage, and I had no intention of doing that. It would have been hard to explain why a tame animal had to be carried around in a cage like a wild one, and of course my friends assumed Chippy was tame, the way a puppy or a kitten is tame. I let it go at that. If I had told them how it really was, they would have said, "But what about all those cute stories you told us about her in the beginning? She was tame then, wasn't she? Well, if she was tame then, why isn't she tame now?"

What could I say?

Later, after I had read a few accounts in books and newspapers by people who had raised squirrels and had talked to a couple of people myself who had gone through the experience, I realized that all of this was an old story. Sooner or later they had all said more or less the same thing: "It was adorable when it was a baby, but then all of a sudden it turned mean." Or "got wild." Or "began acting real violent." And they had all been baffled. They couldn't figure out how anything that had been so tame before could have gotten so untame in such a hurry.

The explanation is that when baby squirrels get taken home by people they know instinctively that their only hope for survival is to accept the situation and trust that they will be treated gently and fed properly. They relax and have faith and try to be as nice as they can and since they're very pretty to look at and very soft and warm and cuddly anyway, their owners think that as they get older all that will happen is that they'll get more lovable. Then comes the sudden change, and the disillusionment. It isn't that they start acting out of character, but in character. They began to feel that they can shift for themselves, so they start being themselves.

But until you realize the intensity of the wildness in the hearts of squirrels you can't understand squirrels and I didn't realize it then any more than the people in the books and the newspapers and the ones I had talked to had, so I was just as baffled by my squirrel as they had been with theirs.

Luckily, there was another side of me that didn't mind Chippy not being a pet, that really admired her for so steadfastly insisting on being what she was and so uncompromisingly refusing to be what she wasn't. And it was this other side of me that kept me from being angry with her really, even sitting there with my wounds still fresh upon me, and that kept me from deciding on the spot that there couldn't possibly be any future for us under the same roof if this was how it was going to be.

I looked up at her again. She had gotten tired of nibbling at the bread and was hiding it in a corner of the molding up at the top of the cabinet. I could see her tail waving and her rump bobbing as she vigorously knocked the crust into the corner with her nose. Then I heard her nails scraping lightly across the wood as she pulled in leaves to cover it up. When that was accomplished she came to the edge of the cabinet and looked down at me eagerly. I knew that what she wanted to do next was jump on my shoulder. When squirrels are getting ready to make a long leap they triangulate on what they're going to leap at by moving their heads back and forth and up and down and around in little circles very rapidly while staring at it bug-eyed. If you're the intended target it can be unnerving.

I was in no mood. I said, "Not now, Chips," and shifted to a chair out of her range.

She immediately turned and ran back to the wall and climbed up onto the picture molding. Perhaps I should explain the term. Most new houses don't have picture moldings, but this was an old house and a lot of old houses have a strip of molding about two inches wide with a raised lip in the front that goes around the walls in some of the rooms at a height of about seven feet. Rather than banging nails in the walls when they wanted to hang pictures, people used to hang them by wires attached to fittings that hooked over the lip of the molding. Thus the name. Anyway, Chippy had soon discovered that although the moldings were narrow she could run along them with the greatest of ease, and she used them as her highways in the sky connecting her favorite eyries on the tops of cabinets and bookcases.

93

She dashed along the molding behind me and I heard her hop down onto the top of the cupboard over the stove. Without having to turn around I knew what was coming next. Chippy had run over to the cupboard because it was closer than the cabinet to the chair I was sitting in now and she knew that she could hit me from there. I could have changed chairs again but I knew that if I had she would have scampered back to the cabinet and we would have been right back where we had started. So I waited, and an instant later she sailed through the air and landed on my left shoulder. Then she started running all over me, trying to get me to play the game in which she jumped on me from the cupboard and then I got up and took her back to the cupboard and she jumped on me again, and so on. But I didn't succumb this time because I still was not in the mood and I really didn't approve of the game anyway. It was too dangerous. Chippy had missed me a couple of times when I had moved at the last instant and upset her calculations and had hurtled past me to the floor almost breaking her neck, and occasionally I had turned my head when I shouldn't have and had wound up with long scratches across my face from her back claws.

When she saw that I wasn't going to play with her she hopped down to the floor and scooted into the living room. For a while I saw her racing around in there checking up on all of the seeds that she had been hiding in the rug before. But then there was silence, and silences were foreboding when she was off somewhere by herself.

Finally I felt that I had better go and see what she was up to. I didn't see her at first when I went into the living room, but I was used to that. It was one of the facts of my life with Chippy that I could come into a room where I knew she was and look right at her and not see her. Of course a squirrel is almost impossible to see even when you're looking right at it out in the woods, but in a room in a house too they have a way of disappearing into whatever background you happen to look at them against that can be rather mystifying.

I stood in the middle of the room, looking all around me and listening. Even after several minutes I still neither heard nor saw anything of Chippy. She could have been anywhere—under the couch or behind the piano, a lamp, the curtains, or she might not have been in the living room any longer at all. She could slip like a shadow from room to room and as you stood looking around for her in one room, she could be getting into serious trouble in another one. And when I say serious trouble I don't just mean knocking things over, although squirrel-precipitated landslides of books, magazines, dishes, condiments, and canned goods were bad enough. She also wanted to gnaw on everything in sight in order to keep her two long lower teeth properly filed down. A squirrel has to keep its lower teeth filed down because they never stop growing and if they're allowed to grow too long they begin to curl back and become useless for gnawing and the squirrel will die of starvation. So Chippy gnawed at the piano and the piano keys, the tables, the chairs, the walls, the woodwork, the telephone and the telephone book, the floor, the refrigerator, the stove, and the radio.

I went into the bedroom to see if Chippy might have slipped in there. When that didn't turn up anything I went back and checked the kitchen. She wasn't there either. Finally I sat down on the couch in the living room. I just kept sitting there until I happened to find myself looking at the tall bookcase and thinking vaguely that something seemed to be out of place. Then I saw Chippy on the third shelf down from the top in a small space between two long rows of books. She looked like a little gnome sitting there staring at me quizzically as if she couldn't understand why I hadn't been able to see her perfectly well all the time.

I went over and held my elbow out to her and she hopped on and rode across the room on my shoulder. I got her special squirrel brush—which actually was an old toothbrush—from the window sill and went back to the couch and sat down again. I held up the brush for Chippy to sniff and she slid down the front of my shirt and sprawled on my leg with her chin on my knee and her arms and legs hanging loose around my leg and her tail down flat behind her. I brushed her for a long time. She liked that and sometimes, after a while, her eyes, which were always so wide wide open, would seem to get dreamy and would even close a little.

Sixteen

Toward the end of October—for reasons that are unimportant here—I started having to be away from home all day and sometimes far into the night five or six days a week. This went on until the beginning of December. Of course it meant that Chippy had to spend her days alone.

At first I thought of asking my sister, who lived fairly near, to keep her at her house until my life returned to normal, but knowing Chippy as I did I decided in the end that she would much rather be alone all day in her own corner of my house where everything was familiar than in a strange place full of strangers.

In the mornings before I left I cleaned her cage and gave her a fresh supply of food and water and just hoped that she would be all right. I knew that she would probably be lonesome at times, but I also knew that she had plenty of birds and cats to spy on out of her windows and the wind to smell and that she had her running and the hiding of her seeds to do whether I was there or not. It turned a little cooler then, which helped, and, at last, there were all kinds of hard-shelled nuts in the stores.

I remember well Chippy's first pecans. I had waited so long for them and then one morning I was driving past an open-air fruit and vegetable stand and saw a sign blowing in the breeze that said, "New Crop Pecans." I stopped and walked over to a man who was emptying sacks of pecans onto a counter.

"Are those really fresh?" I asked.

"You better believe it," he said.

He took two pecans in his palm and cracked one against the other very professionally. "Look at that," he said, holding up the cracked pecan under my nose. "Just look at all that oil. Smell it? Feel it between your fingers. That's what you call a grade-A pecan, mister. How many pounds do you want?"

I said I would take two pounds and as he was giving me my change, he said, "Goddamn squirrels are really giving me a fit today."

"Squirrels?" I said.

He glanced up at the oak tree that shaded his stand. "Up there," he said. "You can't see them, but they're up there. They're coming from miles around now because they can smell these pecans. Every time I turn my back one of them will run down and steal one."

"They must really like pecans," I said.

"You better believe it," he said.

I could hardly wait to get home that night because I kept thinking of the big surprise Chippy had in store for her. It was long after dark by the time I got home and of course Chippy was in her house, but I knew that, as usual, she had heard me coming, because when I went over to her cage I found her looking out of her doorway, waiting for me. I always opened her cage and let her out as soon as I got home. Usually she was drowsy and docile at night and let me hold her in my hands and pet her, but this time she started acting excited as soon as she smelled my hands. She began running all over me, smelling me and searching me.

I had put the bag of pecans on the kitchen table on my way in. I went back to the kitchen with Chippy riding along on my shoulder. I took a pecan out of the bag and held it out in front of me on the flat of my palm. Chippy, perched on my shoulder, saw the pecan, but even though the smell must have been intoxicating, she was wary of it. She gave it a good long looking-over, and then started inching down my arm toward it.

This was a significant moment. How could I not have sensed it? Why didn't something tell me? But I was oblivious. I had no idea of how deeply squirrels feel about hard-shelled nuts, how fanatical they are on the subject, how terribly much they mean to them.

There I was, in all innocence, without the least premonition of the misery that was going to be visited on me eventually as a direct consequence of my having brought home the first sack of pecans to my squirrel, saying, "Come on, Chips. You're going to like this. Come on, now. It won't bite you."

Down my arm she came, quivering all over with anticipation, nose and whiskers going a mile a minute. Finally she reached the pecan. She sniffed one end and then hooked her nose around and took a quick sniff of the other end. Then she picked up the pecan in her teeth by one end. It made her look rather like a man with the end of a football stuck in his mouth.

She sat up in my palm and began spinning the pecan

rapidly in her hands and sniffing it as it spun. Then she ran back up to my shoulder with it in her mouth, paused there to spin it a little more, hopped onto the back of a chair and from there jumped down to the floor.

I reached down to try to pick her up but she eluded me and shot across the floor and disappeared into the living room. When I followed her in there I found her sitting on the couch, spinning the pecan again. As soon as I came near her she darted away to the back of an armchair. She stayed there just long enough to spin the pecan some more, and then she jumped over to a table, sailed across it and made a spectacular leap to the side of her cage. She hurried up to the top of the cage and began spinning and sniffing again, and what she reminded me of now was a man who has picked up a satchel on the sidewalk and discovered that it's stuffed full of money. All she seemed to want to do was get off by herself somewhere where nobody could see her and run her fingers through it.

Of course I was pleased that my present was such a big hit with her, but I couldn't figure out why she didn't crack the pecan and eat it. I stood below her, looking up and watching her spinning the pecan, and I noticed that every once in a while she would pause and scrape it slightly with her lower teeth. It occurred to me that what she was doing was checking the shell for flaws. At first I thought she was trying to find a thin spot or a hairline crack where she could best begin the job of opening the shell, but later I realized that that wasn't it. She was checking the shell for flaws all right, but the point was that if she found it was perfect then it would be a treasure of fantastic value to her because it would mean she could store it away and it would last indefinitely.

I began to get the idea after Chippy had hidden the first pecan under the log at the bottom of her cage and then had run back out to the kitchen and hopped up onto the table and gotten another one out of the bag and had gone through the whole performance again, and then had done the same thing with half a dozen more. That was when I decided that I had to put a stop to it and went to the kitchen myself and got two pecans and cracked one against the other in my palm, just as I had seen the man do. The next time Chippy came running back for another pecan I gave her half of the cracked one. It had the effect that I wanted. For the first time she seemed interested in finding out what a pecan actually tasted like.

She perched on the back of a chair and began stripping away the remainder of the shell from the pecan, and I was impressed with what a quick, neat, precise and generally surgical job she did of it. She ate the half of the nut I had given her down to the last crumb and when I handed her the other half she stripped that and ate it too. Then she started for the bag again. I snatched it away just in time and put it on top of the refrigerator, where it was completely out of her reach, because I had a feeling that if I had let her she would have hidden the whole rest of the two pounds of pecans before she was through.

As it was—thwarted—she ran back to the living room and started the endless business of digging up all of the pecans that she had already hidden and hiding them again. She kept it up until she made the mistake of going into her cage to check on the pecan under the log. I pulled the screen across the top, locking her in, and said good night and turned off the lights.

After that it was the deluge—brazils, walnuts, almonds, more pecans, filberts, hazelnuts, chestnuts, and cashews. I brought them home by the bagful, and Chippy would eat one and hide eight, eat one and hide fifteen, and so on. It got so that it seemed that you couldn't pick up anything in the house without finding a nut hidden under it, even though I was trying my best to keep up with the situation by going around and collecting as many of them as I could find without Chippy noticing and returning them to stock.

Now, looking back on it, I should have known what was going to come of it all. There was a frenzy about the way Chippy acted around those nuts that should have been a clear warning to me, but I guess I was getting such a kick out of her getting such a kick out of the nuts that I refused to let any dark thoughts spoil the fun.

Seventeen

Early one morning during this period—the several weeks when I had to leave Chippy alone almost every day—I was awakened from a sound sleep by an alarming discord. It was not that the noise was so loud or that it was entirely unfamiliar that brought me straight up in bed, but that the source of it seemed to be within the house itself. It was the scolding of a squirrel, and I was pretty sure that it was coming from the living room.

I had a sinking feeling that I knew what must have happened. Lately, squirrels had been jumping over from the sapodilla tree outside Chippy's window to her window sill and making a great nuisance of themselves. At first I had thought that they were doing it because they had discovered that there was a squirrel living in my house and they had wanted to visit with her through the screen, but finally I had realized it was because they had caught wind of Chippy's sunflower seeds and hard-shelled nuts and they had wanted to get in the house and take them away from her. I had seen them run back and forth along the window sill and climb all over the screen looking for an opening or a weak place where they could come through, and a couple of times they had actually gnawed at the wooden frame of the screen until I had chased them away. Now I thought that they must have been working on the frame constantly while I had been gone every day and had finally succeeded in making a hole and one of them was in the living room this minute.

I hurried out to the living room, trying to clear my mind to deal with what I thought was going to be a very ticklish situation. Chippy was one thing. A big squirrel from outdoors was quite another. I wondered how I would get it out of the house. It would probably attack me if it began to feel cornered and I knew that I had better take care not to get it to feeling that way because if Chippy could cut me up so bad when she got a little annoyed with me, what could a big squirrel do?

The scolding stopped when I entered the living room. I looked first of all at Chippy in her cage and saw that she was very excited. She was perched high up on one of her branches and her tail was flicking and her back feet were drumming. I took a quick look around the room but I couldn't see another squirrel anywhere. I thought it must have hidden when it had heard me coming and I looked at Chippy again to see where she was looking because I knew that if there was another squirrel in the room she would know where it was and would be looking in that direction. But the strange thing was that she seemed to be looking out her window. That didn't make sense to me because I was almost positive that the racket I had heard had come from the living room. I went to the window and looked out too, trying to see what she saw.

I couldn't see anything. There were no cats on the lawn down below, no squirrels in the sapodilla. There wasn't even a cardinal flitting about looking for spiders under the eaves. I was standing right beside Chippy's cage with her not more than a foot from my left ear when all of a sudden the scolding started again. I jumped because it was so close and so loud. Then I looked around at where it was coming from and couldn't believe my eyes or my ears. It was coming out of my little squirrel.

I just stood there and stared at her as the caterwauling continued. Chippy had never made a sound above a murmur in all the time that I had known her and here she was now carrying on like a fishwife. I was appalled, but I could see plainly that she was having a very fine time.

It went on and on. Finally I sat down to wait for her to get it out of her system, but I knew that it might take quite a while. I had noticed in the past that once squirrels start scolding they are reluctant to stop. And I had also noticed that after they've been at it for a half hour or so they seem to have forgotten completely whatever it was that set them off and are just going on with it for the fun of it. I was pretty sure that that was how it was with Chippy. A cat or a squirrel or a cardinal may have provoked her into such a performance in the beginning, but now she was simply infatuated with the sound of her own voice.

And I must say, in all frankness, that a squirrel's voice is not a thing of overwhelming beauty. It is reedy, erratic, tuneless, and derivative. A girl I know, listening to a squirrel in a tree nearby one day, said, "You know, I hate to say it, but they sound sort of like a duck."

They do sound sort of like a duck, although I'm sure

they think they sound sort of like a tiger. They also sound sort of like one of those little horns you blow on New Year's Eve. Anyway, Chippy kept on with her scolding until she finally wound down. Then she went into her house, curled up, pulled her tail over her eyes and went to sleep, obviously feeling very pleased with herself. For my own part, I couldn't help wondering if this would be going on all the time from now on. Actually, months went by afterwards without a peep from Chippy. It got to be rather like waiting for the other shoe to drop. Now that I knew that she could do it I kept waiting for her to do it again. I think that I even began to want very badly for her to do it again. But Chippy, having spoken, appeared to feel that she had said it all.

Eighteen

It was also during this period when I had to be away from home so much of the time that I tried a daring social experiment; I should have known better. It began with a brainstorm that I had one morning when I was at the local pet shop buying a fresh supply of sunflower seeds. I happened to wander to the back of the store, where they kept small animals in cages, and as I stood looking at some hamsters it occurred to me that one of them might be good company for Chippy. I didn't know anything about them but they looked harmless, inoffensive, and amenable.

I dismissed the idea immediately, thinking that Chippy would never go for it, but then, when I was having a cup of coffee at the drugstore, I started thinking about it again. I had been feeling increasingly guilty lately about leaving

Chippy alone and I was willing to do just about anything to try to make up for it. The more I thought about the hamster idea the more it appealed to me, and when I finished my coffee I returned to the pet shop.

There are many different kinds of pet shop owners, of course. Some are very pleasant, some aren't. Some will talk your head off if you give them half a chance, some are taciturn. Some have a sense of humor about what they're doing, some take it too seriously. The owner of this particular shop, Tom Truman, was of the type who treat you as if they cannot for the life of them figure out why a reasonably intelligent-looking person like you would want to waste your time in a place like this.

He looked at me closely when he saw me come back in. The bells on the back of his door always seemed to take a long time to quiet down after you closed the door behind you. When they did, I said, "I thought I might have another look at those hamsters."

"Those what?" Tom said, incredulously.

"Aren't those hamsters back there, Tom?" I asked, pointing to the cage at the back of the shop.

He scratched his head and gave me a funny look, glancing back and forth from one of my eyes to the other.

"Hamsters," he said. "That's right."

"I was looking at them before."

He shrugged. "Well, some people like them," he said.

I edged past him and went and looked at the hamsters again. There were about a dozen of them in the cage. Some were asleep while others were nibbling at pieces of lettuce and fruit and others were rushing headlong all over the place. The ones that were rushing about climbed right over the ones that were sleeping and the ones that were nibbling just as if they were part of the landscape and bumped into each other and bounced off and kept on going.

As I stood there looking at them I was trying to envisage one of them living in Chippy's cage with Chippy. On the one hand I could see Chippy being overjoyed to have a little friend to play with, but on the other hand I could see her thinking of the hamster as an intruder, a rival for her food, an enemy. In that case, what would she do to it? Intimidate it? Beat it up? Perhaps even kill it?

"Want one?" Tom asked, disbelievingly.

"I don't know," I said. "How much are they?"

"A dollar each."

"What do they eat?"

"Damn near anything," Tom said. "You name it, they eat it."

I tried to imagine the scene the way it would be if I took a hamster home with me. I saw myself lifting up one side of Chippy's cage and slipping the hamster under. Then I could see Chippy coming down from the upper regions of her cage to find out what that fuzzy little thing down there was, and advancing on it the way she always did on anything that was unfamiliar to her: circling warily—tail pulled around as a shield, back feet hooked around backwards to facilitate a rapid retreat should that prove necessary, belly dragging the ground—fixing the hamster with one big eye and then the other, ducking in to give it a quick sniff and then ducking back and circling some more.

"I wonder how one of them would get along with my squirrel," I said.

Tom shook his head. "That would be kind of hard to say. They might get along real good, but then again they might not."

"That's what I was thinking," I said.

"Your squirrel might be jealous of it."

"That's right," I said. "And even if they did get so they

would play together, I'm afraid my squirrel would be too rough for a little thing like that."

All in all, it seemed to me that the idea had a much better chance of failing than of succeeding and that in the process of failing it could cause everyone concerned a lot of grief. The hamsters all looked very contented there in the cage, and, probably, Tom would eventually sell all of them to people who would give them a good home. Chippy was getting along all right just as she was and a hamster in her cage might upset her whole life. And as for me, basically, I didn't want any more animals in the house anyway.

"I guess I'll just forget about it, Tom," I said.

But that afternoon when I returned to the village on some sort of errand, I thought about the hamsters again and before I knew what I was doing I found myself going back into the pet shop.

"I think I'll take a chance on it after all, Tom," I said.

He gave me another of his looks—this time as if he really had very serious doubts about me. Then he put a hamster into a cardboard hamster carrying case, took my dollar, and wished me luck.

It was around four o'clock when I got home. Chippy had been playing hard all afternoon and she was asleep in her house. I sat down on the floor beside the cage and let the hamster out of the box. It looked a little bit like a squirrel, except that it had no tail and was brown and white instead of gray and silver and had tiny shiny eyes instead of great big shiny ones. Also, the backs of its hands and feet were naked, whereas a squirrel's are covered with fur. It didn't seem to be all that bright either. It went around in circles on the floor until I put a piece of lettuce that I managed to fish out from between the bars of the cage in its path. Then it stopped going in circles and started eating. Every time it ran out of something to eat it started going in circles again. It didn't seem to be interested in who I was or where it was or what was going to happen to it from now on. All it was interested in was eating.

"Chipper," I said, looking up toward the house at the top of the cage. "I've got a little pal here for you."

Not the slightest movement or sound came from the house. All I could see of Chippy was a fluff of tail across the doorway.

"Come on out and see who's here, Chips," I said.

Still there was no reaction from the house. That was strange because I knew Chippy had heard me come home and I had a feeling she was aware of the presence of the hamster. For a creature as curious about everything as she, it was a most unusual thing for her not to investigate the situation right away.

Slowly and cautiously I lifted up one side of the cage and put the hamster under. Inside the cage it went in circles until it bumped into the log. Then it started climbing all over the log. I knew it was impossible that Chippy hadn't felt me lift up the cage and that she didn't hear the hamster skittering around on the log, and yet she didn't stir. Then the hamster made the mistake of digging out some of the sunflower seeds that Chippy had hidden in the newspaper on the floor and suddenly there was a flurry up in the house. First an eye appeared at one of the windows. Then Chippy stuck her head out of the doorway. I thought she looked very stern.

"There's somebody down here who wants to meet you, Gray," I said.

Chippy emerged from her house and crept out a little way on the branch directly below her porch. She tilted her head sharply over to one side and looked down at the hamster with one eye. The hamster paid no attention to her whatsoever but kept right on snuffling around among her hidden treasures. Chippy tilted her head the other way so that she could look at the hamster with the other eye.

"This is your new little pal, Mouse," I said. "I think you two are going to have marvelous times together. Why don't you come down and get acquainted?"

Chippy just continued to study the hamster and I began to be afraid that all of a sudden she might go into action and beat the living daylights out of the hamster for daring to meddle in her private affairs. But what she did do was completely unanticipated. When she got through staring at the hamster she turned and hopped back up onto her porch. There she paused and looked at me as if to say, "I'm going back to bed now. When I come out again I expect that thing down there to have departed, never to return." Then she disappeared into her house.

"Well, you didn't have to be so stuffy about it," I said. "You could have come down and said hello anyway."

But I knew the game was over. I put the hamster back into its carrying case and by breaking the speed laws managed to reach the pet shop before it closed. I gave the hamster to Tom, saying that I didn't want a refund or anything but just asked that he take it back now and make a special effort to see that it got a good home, and that was that.

Nineteen

In November it is often as hot during the day as it has been straight through since May, but at night it is usually quite cool. By December the hot days are outnumbered by the cool ones and you begin to feel that life may be worth living after all, and from then on until the inferno begins again every day is precious.

In December I started carrying Chippy in her cage down to the terrace for a few hours a couple of afternoons a week. She had not been out of the house since the day she had hidden in the hole in the log, but she seemed to feel secure in her cage and it was obvious that she enjoyed the sun and the cool wind and being surrounded by nature. And she liked digging in the grass in the cracks between the coral rock paving stones on the terrace.

She usually had plenty of company because there were

always many birds in the vicinity of the terrace, both the regular crowd and the ones that had come down for the winter. The winter visitors were mostly various kinds of warblers, painted buntings and shy catbirds. At first all of the birds were apprehensive about the cage being on the terrace and they stayed deep back in the foliage, watching the cage and Chippy running around inside it, but soon they got used to it and went about their bathing and fluttering around the feeder as usual. In fact, after a while, the cardinals and blue jays began to get excited the minute they saw me lugging the great cage down the steps to the terrace because I always put a handful of seeds on the ground inside the cage for Chippy to bury in the grass and they knew that they could usually steal a few by darting in when her back was turned and snatching them out from between the bars. Chippy didn't really seem to mind this filching on the part of the birds. The only thing that disturbed her was when they walked around on the screen on top of her cage. She would run up and try to sniff their feet. When they saw her coming and got alarmed and flew away, she would cling to the side of the cage and look after them with her nose stuck through the bars as if to say, "Come back! I won't hurt you! I only want to smell your feet!"

Of all of the birds that came to the terrace—resident and visitor—none were as beautiful and fascinating as the spotted-breasted orioles. I wasn't even aware of the existence of the species until one summer when I began to notice quite often a pair of orange and black birds about the size of jays flitting through the trees around the terrace. Then I began occasionally to see others just like them all over town. I knew that they must have been some kind of oriole but I didn't think that there were orioles of any kind in Florida at that time of year. When I asked people what kind of birds they were most of them had no idea, but a few said that they thought they were called Guatemalan orioles. Finally I looked them up in a bird book and found out that they were called spotted-breasted orioles, but that they had indeed originally come from Central America. The book said that they had been introduced into Florida in 1949 when a mated pair escaped from a cage aboard a ship unloading bananas in the Miami River. They found the area agreeable and the species has been proliferating and spreading out ever since.

They are bright orange, with black masks and bibs, black wings streaked with white, black tails and black flecks on their breasts. They are astonishingly communicative, and I mean not only that they talk a lot among themselves but that they will talk to you too if you will take the trouble to learn how to imitate the *tch-tch-tch* sound that they make in ordinary conversation. They have two different songs that I know of. One is cheerful and pretty. The other is one, long, poignant, gradually rising note that I seem to hear out of them only on rainy days when they sit on the telephone wire over the terrace and mope and in moments of great anxiety. But they go *tch-tch-tch* all the time.

They live in mated pairs and the two birds of a pair almost always are close together, within a few feet of each other, actually. When you see one you may not see the other immediately, but if you look closely you will usually see it nearby. If they happen to be feeding in trees some distance apart you will hear them talking back and forth to each other—*tch-tch-tch, tch-tch-tch*—always letting each other know where they are and what they're up to. When one of them discovers something very exciting to eat and wants its mate to share it, it starts making the *tch-tch-tch* rapidly and continuously and with a slightly hysterical lilt at the end of each phrase.

I think they eat mostly fruit and insects and they seem to prefer to stay high off the ground. At least you seldom see them feeding on the ground. When I first began to see them I hoped that they would come to the feeder that I had hung on a low branch over the terrace, but they weren't interested in the wild birdseed that I kept in the feeder for the blue jays and cardinals and painted buntings. I called the Audubon Society and they said that spotted-breasted orioles are extraordinarily fond of any kind of pastry, particularly doughnuts. So I started putting crumbled doughnuts on the window sill outside the window where I usually did my typing and soon the orioles began hanging around the terrace all the time. In fact it seemed that whenever I came out the door they would be there in the bougainvillaea waiting for me and clucking at me passionately and I would have to go back inside and get a doughnut for them and crumble it up on the window sill. If they weren't waiting for me when I went outside to take a walk they would spot me sooner or later from high up in some tree and cluck at me until I clucked back and when I got back to the house they would be there waiting for me. If I stayed in the house and ignored them for a while they would sit in a tree outside the room where I was and cluck at me through the window and if I tried to elude them by going to another room they would be at the window in there a moment later with their *tch-tch-tch*.

It didn't take me long to find out that almost all of the birds on God's green earth are extraordinarily fond of doughnuts. The blue jays loved them, the cardinals loved them, the mockingbirds, crows, catbirds, buntings and sparrows loved them. Even the red-bellied woodpeckers loved them. This presented certain problems. I suddenly found myself buying a dozen powdered-sugar doughnuts a day at my local supermarket and still forever seeming to be getting caught short.

Furthermore, it soon became terribly apparent that squirrels also were crazy about doughnuts. I had had my troubles with them before in the matter of the birdseed in the feeder and had had to resort to devious tricks to keep them from it, but there seemed to be no way to keep them from the doughnuts. They listened for the special tone in the orioles' clucking that meant that I had just come outside with a doughnut in my hand and they started racing through the trees for the house. They could easily jump from the trellis to the doughnut window sill and I would hear a great beating of wings and indignant scolding of blue jays and look out the window and see the squirrels triumphantly wolfing doughnut. Frankly, I wouldn't have minded them eating a little doughnut now and then if they had been orderly and fair about it, but they weren't. They were disorderly and greedy, and once they got on the window sill they wouldn't allow so much as a single sparrow to come and share the wealth with them. Which meant that I would have to go out and chase them away and that they would come back five minutes later and then I would have to go and do it again, which can wear you down after a while.

Chippy was largely indifferent to the squabbling over the doughnuts. In the first place, she couldn't understand what the birds and the squirrels saw in them anyway. She didn't like them much herself. When she was on the terrace and I brought out a doughnut for the birds I would always offer her a piece first because she would go out of her mind bouncing back and forth in her cage if I didn't. Usually she would sniff the doughnut eagerly and then lose interest right away and go back to her seeds, but occasionally she would take the piece that I offered her, make a big production out of sniffing it and examining it and taking a few nibbles of it, and then simply pull her hands apart and let it fall to the ground. It hurts me to say it, but I have a feeling that the only reason she ever took any doughnut at all was (1) to show the birds that were standing around knocking themselves out clucking and peeping and whistling that she was always offered the doughnut first and could have eaten the whole thing if she had felt like it, and (2) to keep that much of it at least away from them.

Which made me often wonder, did the other squirrels really like doughnuts as much as they seemed to? Or were they, also, interested mostly in keeping as much as possible away from the birds? I had my doubts. Squirrels have a deep streak of competitiveness in them where birds are concerned and they always seem to be ready to go to a lot of trouble to remind them of who is truly boss of the trees.

But maybe they really did like doughnuts immoderately. If so, it wasn't the only thing I had noticed that they liked and Chippy didn't, and vice versa. For instance, they liked peanut butter. Chippy could take it or leave it. She had begun to love raw corn on the cob, but when, as an experiment, I tried to give some to the outdoor squirrels, they gave me a funny look and turned their noses up at it, and they couldn't abide lettuce or honeydew melon either.

It was a surprise to me, and something of a disappointment too, that the squirrels that came to the terrace when Chippy was out never paid much attention to her and that she in turn never paid much attention to them. When I first began taking her out I kept waiting for the great moment when a squirrel would spy Chippy and come over to investigate her. I thought it would be like a

couple of strange dogs meeting, a lot of frantic recon-
noitering and then a boisterous coming together with,
perhaps, quacks and nips and nose-rubbings through the
bars. And then, I thought, more squirrels would come
and make friends with her and they would be her regular
playmates and whenever she was out they would come
over and visit with her and all chase each other around
the cage, or something.

It never happened. The squirrels arrived, glanced at
Chippy, if that, and then settled down to the business at
hand, which was scaring off the birds and devouring the
doughnuts. When, rarely, a squirrel would start to come
toward the cage, Chippy would wait until it was quite
close and then would run at it across the ground or down
the side of her cage and it would dash away and not come
back. Usually. But one day when I had gone into the
house for a minute, I heard a horrendous squealing from
the terrace. I ran outside and found Chippy, who was doing the squealing, plastered upside down to the screen
at the top of her cage while down at the bottom a squirrel
was reaching through the bars and raking out her sunflower seeds as fast as it could. I chased the squirrel away
and told Sarah Bernhardt that she could come down now.

In late spring and early summer when the birds were
having their babies the activity on the terrace reached a
crescendo. I think that the first thing the parent birds did
when their babies learned to fly was to lead them over
to the terrace to show them where the water and the
doughnuts were. I had my hands full keeping doughnuts
on the window sill and water in the birdbath because the
blue jays, mockingbirds and woodpeckers came in
droves and their fat babies sat in rows on the trellis and
on the branches overhead and wailed pathetically until
their mothers jammed some doughnut down their
throats, and the balustrade and the ground all around

the birdbath were always soaked with water from all the bathing that went on.

Ordinarily only one pair of cardinals and one pair of spotted-breasted orioles were in residence on the entire three acres of land on which the house I live in stands. This was because these two species of birds have it in common that—unlike blue jays and mockingbirds and woodpeckers and all of the other kinds of birds that I know anything about—they will not tolerate any other birds of their own kind in their territory. They gang up on invaders and harass them mercilessly until they succeed in driving them away—except during the nesting season, when the trees around my house were always filled with strange pairs of orioles and cardinals. However, even then my two cardinals and my two orioles were not so generous that they would let any of their visiting relations near the terrace. Their rule seemed to be, the trees and the grounds perhaps, but the doughnuts and the birdbath definitely not. Unfortunately this policy of exclusion often led to some trying moments. When the cardinal and oriole babies were a couple of months out of the nest their parents started urging them to move along. Usually the young birds left without too much of a fuss but sometimes a few of them would resist and try to keep on hanging around after their time. Their parents would have to get very nasty with them before they were able to drive them away.

I don't know why cardinals are like that, but I believe that the orioles chase their young away because they know in their hearts that they're a very rare bird in their present surroundings and they want to increase the chances for the survival of their species by spreading themselves out as far and as fast as they can. I found the whole process pretty sad because young orioles are one of the most appealing creatures in the world and I hated to see them go each year. The first time I saw one I didn't know what it was. I saw it through the kitchen window early one morning, hopping about in the bougainvillaea. It was a little puff of canary yellow with pale gray wings and it kept making a high-pitched plaintive tweet that sounded like someone blowing on a muted police whistle. When I went outside to get a better look at it I saw the two big orioles perched above it on a high swaying branch of the bougainvillaea and I made the connection.

After that the baby oriole came to the terrace all the time. Like his parents he was very friendly and loved doughnuts and talked to me constantly in his high whistle. I was just getting used to seeing him around when one day about two weeks later I went out on the terrace and saw two little orioles sitting side by side on the trellis. A little brother, or sister! A couple of weeks after that a third one appeared! Later I found out that orioles always have three babies but at intervals of a couple of weeks and not all at once like most other birds. After about two months the baby orioles began to look less like little round balls of yellow fluff and more like proper spotted-breasted orioles. Their necks grew longer and underneath the yellow feathers you could see the black of their masks and bibs starting to show through. At that point their parents began the unhappy business of trying to make them go away. Sometimes I would see the two parent birds and one of the young birds sitting close together up in a tree and they would all be making the poignant sound that I spoke of before at each other. Finally both parents would attack the little bird at once and it would fly away to another tree and they would follow it and the whole thing would start all over again. And then after a while I would just never see the little orioles around any more and the big orioles would start acting more relaxed, and I would know that the cycle had been completed again. But each summer when my orioles brought me their first baby and sat in the bougainvillaea clucking proudly at me while I clucked enthusiastically back at them to let them know that I thought the kid looked great, I couldn't help thinking of the time coming when they would all be sitting in a tree together making that mournful sound at each other.

Twenty

All winter and all spring Chippy kept on storing away nuts. If I gave her ten she would run around the house until they were all safely hidden. That was today. To-morrow it would be ten more. Once in a while she would interrupt her running around to crack a nut and eat it and sometimes late at night and early in the morning I would hear her out in the living room in her house crack-ing shells. But for the most part she lived on her sun-flower seeds and lettuce and just about all of the pounds and pounds of hard-shelled nuts that I brought home to her disappeared into hundreds of hiding places all over the house.

I kept hoping as it went on that eventually she would reach a saturation point, when she would say to herself, "Well, I guess that ought to do it. That should be enough." But apparently there was no such thing as enough. For example, besides hiding nuts all over the house, she also stuffed so many into her own house that they started coming out the windows, and the floor was so thickly covered with nuts and broken pieces of shell that when she went to bed it was like a person curling up and going to sleep on a mattress made of cobblestones and shards.

To add to the problem, she developed a habit of wanting to gnaw on her house all the time. I think that what got her started on it was an innocent desire to enlarge her windows, but it quickly got out of hand. She gnawed a little away from each window and then went back and gnawed a little more. Pretty soon she had gnawed away so much of the wall on one side of her house that what had originally been two small windows became one big window and there was almost nothing left of the wall. She couldn't even turn over in her sleep without sending half a dozen pecans and filberts raining down on the floor. That was all right, but when she started on the windows on the other side and I could see the time coming when she would finally gnaw away the last bit of wall and the whole bottom half of the house would drop like a stone, I decided that it was time for a new house. I made this new house out of much heavier cardboard than the first and made the windows quite big to begin with, hoping that Chippy wouldn't feel that she had to do any remodeling on her own.

But it wasn't long before she had her new house chock full of nuts and the walls half gnawed away and the pecans and the filberts were raining down on the floor again. I built three cardboard houses for Chippy that winter and spring and then one day I realized that this couldn't go on and bought a piece of lumber and took it to my brother-in-law, who has power saws and drills and braces and bits, and got him to build me a house for Chippy like all of her other houses except out of wood an inch thick. She accepted the wooden house as readily as she had all of the others and started right in filling it up with nuts and happily gnawing at the walls and the ceiling and the windows, and I couldn't help wondering how long it was going to take her to reduce the whole thing to sawdust.

As Chippy grew more and more intense about hoarding the nuts that I gave her, she also seemed to grow more and more intense about everything else, particularly the games that she played with me. While the weather was still cool I could wear two or three shirts and two or three pairs of pants when we played, but around the end of April, when it started getting hot again, I couldn't wear all those clothes. I had to restrict our games because she was simply too much for me—too strong, too quick, too violent. When we played she not only cut me with her claws but also gave me some rather serious bites now and then. The fact is that when squirrels play with each other they play very rough, so it was only natural that when Chippy played with me she wanted to play rough too. She wanted to nip my hands the way squirrels nip each other when they chase each other around in the trees but I didn't have all that fur covering my fingers. I tried to stay out of her way when she started getting too rough but sometimes she wouldn't leave me alone, trying to get me to play, and I would have to go to another room and close the door to get away from her. Every time I did that it made me think something was wrong with all of this. I had to be afraid of a little animal that wasn't even one year old and weighed less than two pounds and was supposed to be my pet.

Then one morning in May something genuinely spooky happened. It was a dark morning. I remember it very well. It had been raining steadily for several days and I had put some newspapers on the floor near the kitchen door to drip on when I came into the house soaking wet. When I got up I let Chippy out of her cage and she played on the floor in the kitchen while I sat at the table and had my first cup of coffee of the day. I didn't pay much attention to what she was doing, but I was vaguely aware that she was bringing hard-shelled nuts from somewhere and hiding them under the edges of the newspapers. After a while, when I got up to make myself another cup of coffee, I heard a peculiar sound. It was a faint, mysterious little sound. It seemed to be coming from Chippy but I had never heard her make it before and I couldn't quite believe that she was making it now. I paused and bent over to look at her more closely and then I saw that the sound was indeed coming from her and that she was making it by clicking her front teeth together very rapidly. It seemed like a ridiculous thing for her to be doing. I couldn't understand it. I stood there looking at her bewilderedly. She lay on the floor between me and the newspapers, propped up on her elbows and with her back legs spread wide apart so that her stomach was flat on the floor.

"What's all this supposed to mean, Chip?" I said.

I started to go toward her, intending to squat down in front of her and tease her a little about this weird exhibition that she was putting on.

Suddenly she ran toward me and jumped at my leg. I was wearing long pants but I could feel her claws sink into my calf. She clung there for a moment and then leaped away, and as she did so she kicked at my leg with her back claws. Then she began dashing back and forth in front of me, kicking at my leg each time she went past. I was so astonished by her behavior that I stayed where I was for a minute, letting it happen. Then, at last, I realized Chippy wasn't kidding. She was standing guard over the nuts that she had hidden under the newspapers. Protecting them from me. Me! Who had given her the miserable things in the first place!

I was appalled. I retreated in bad order and sat down at the table and pulled up my pantsleg and looked at my leg. There were some long cuts across my shin that were bleeding nicely. I looked over at Chippy and saw that she had returned to her watchdog position between me and her nuts, and she was clicking ferociously again. We gazed at each other for a while and I guess we both understood very well that our relationship had now entered a new phase. I tried to think what I should do. It seemed to me that I couldn't possibly let Chippy get away with something like this, that I would have to show her once and for all who was boss in my house. But I didn't know how to go about it. When I started to get up Chippy made a quick move toward me and I sat down again. She looked at me defiantly, as if she knew exactly what she was doing and was just daring me to do something about it.

I got up again and she started toward me again, but this time I spoke sternly to her and clapped my hands and she seemed to lose her nerve. She turned and climbed up on a chair, jumped to the window sill, climbed up the screen and hauled herself up to the picture molding, ran halfway around the room on the molding and finally hopped down onto the top of the cabinet in the corner.

From there she looked down at me, and I, thinking that what had happened must surely have been an aberration and would never happen again under any circumstances and not wanting to make the situation any worse than it was, relented and spoke softly to her, saying that if she would forgive me for having yelled and clapped my hands at her, I would forgive her for having clicked at me and scratched my leg.

I went over to the cabinet and held out my arm with

my elbow pointed in her direction and bobbing up and down, the way I always did when I was inviting her to jump down onto my shoulder. She jumped immediately, and ran across my shoulders and down my other arm, which was hanging by my side. On her way down she bit my arm once just above the elbow and then she bit my hand all over four or five times, deeply and fiercely and amazingly quickly.

Again, I was so astonished at what was happening that it took me a moment to react. By then Chippy had run back to the living room and gone into her cage. I had recently made a door on the side of the cage by taking a pair of wire cutters and cutting out a section of the cage roughly a foot high by six inches wide and then reattaching the piece that I had cut away to the cage with clothespins. The two clothespins on the left side of the door served as hinges and the one on the right as a latch. I followed Chippy into the living room and closed her door and fastened it securely. She was very excited and was running around and around in the cage at high speed. Then I went to the bathroom and washed the blood off my hand and arm.

The bites were serious, but the fact of them was beside the point. It was the meaning of them that depressed me terribly. It looked as if Chippy had deliberately set up a situation in which she could pretend that I was trying to steal her nuts so that she would have an excuse to attack me. And the way she had attacked me had been so malicious that it seemed it could only have been done out of pure hatred. That bothered me more than anything else—the thought that down in her heart Chippy hated me. It seemed profoundly unfair.

I sat in the living room in the pale light of the gloomy morning and watched Chippy running around and thought that it was all over now.

Twenty-one

I really didn't see how there was any way that Chippy and I could go on together after what had happened. I didn't feel bitter toward her. I still respected her and admired her and had great affection for her, but I just didn't think that I could ever trust her again. And if I didn't trust her I couldn't let her out of her cage, and, as I have said before, the one thing that was out of the question was that I would keep her in my house as a caged animal.

So I spent the next couple of days trying to figure out the best way to go about returning Chippy to the wild. The cats that were always hanging around on the property were the main problem. On several occasions when I had put Chippy down on the terrace in her cage I had caught one or another of them creeping up on her and had chased it away just as it had been about to pounce. The alarming part of it was that Chippy had never shown the least sign of fear of the cats but had always hung on the bars of her cage and watched them approaching her with enormous interest. Of course it never came to it but I wasn't at all sure that she would have run away if one of the cats had ever succeeded in getting close enough to launch itself at her, and a cat could have done her a lot of damage if it had been able to get its claws into her through the bars. It was obvious that the cats truly fascinated her and that she would have loved to investigate them thoroughly, and perhaps play with them. In fact one day when I brought her a very small black kitten and held it up for her next to her cage just to see how she would act, she stuck her long nose through the bars eagerly and couldn't get enough of sniffing the kitten's fur, and when I gave her one of its paws through the bars she set to work right away trimming its toenails with her teeth just the way she did her own.

At any rate, I was afraid that if I turned Chippy loose in the oak trees across the field from my house she would see a cat prowling in the grass down below one day and go down to make friends and that would be the end of her.

Therefore I tried to think of some other place where I could let her go, and while I was doing all this pondering and worrying I kept her locked up in her cage, and she apparently had no idea why. She seemed to have forgotten all about the incident in the kitchen. It might never have happened at all to see the way she looked at me with such innocence every time I passed by her cage. She clung to the bars near the door, begging to be let out, and finally I broke down and obliged her.

She was wildly happy to be free again. When I sat down on the floor she rolled over and over on the rug in front of me and turned somersaults, and she even stood up on her hind legs and did the funny little dance that she always did when she wanted to show me that she was particularly happy. Then she ran ecstatically all through the house and, at last, came back to me and stretched out on my knee for her brushing.

And so, for a while at least, I stopped thinking about letting Chippy go. I stopped because it was easier not to think about it than it was to think about it, easier to forget about the way she had attacked me than to brood about it, easier to let things slide rather than make the decisions that I knew very well would have to be made sooner or later.

Things went on as before until we were in the middle of July, and then one morning Chippy attacked me again.

This time I was sitting in the living room reading a letter when she abruptly stopped running around hiding her nuts to fly at me and bite my arm. When I sprang away from her she sprang after me and bit me a second time. There was nothing I could do but run to the bathroom and close the door between us. I stood there looking at the blood on the doorjamb where my arm had brushed against it. Then I opened the door a crack and looked at Chippy lying in front of it, daring me to come out, and I remember closing the door again and sitting down on the toilet seat and thinking that things indeed had come to a pretty pass when I could be held captive in my own bathroom by a squirrel.

Time went by and I just kept on sitting there, feeling very depressed. When I finally got up and looked out into the living room again, I saw that Chippy had gone back to her cage. I hurried over and fastened the door. Then I looked at her and she looked back with her teeth clicking menacingly, and for the first and only time in my whole experience with Chippy I lost my temper. Something about that defiant face, those bright eyes, those chattering teeth infuriated me. I clapped my hands very loudly right in front of her. I knew that it would terrify her and I knew that it was a truly unsporting thing to do when she was locked up in her cage and I had her completely in my power. She did what I thought she would do. She started racing around hysterically, moving so fast that she was almost a blur. I immediately regretted what I had done, and I regret it even now. But that didn't do any good at the time, and Chippy ran until she was too exhausted to run any more.

When it was all over, I felt convinced that in her own way, through her explosive fits of meanness, Chippy was trying to tell me something, and that what she was trying to tell me was that it was time for her to go.

As if to make the point even clearer, her behavior from then on began to be impossible. She gradually got so mean that I couldn't let her out of her cage any more, except once in a while at night, when she tended to be a bit more civil. All day she clicked her teeth at me, and to that unpleasant sound she added another, a sort of low infuriated moaning that I took to express a seething hatred, and between the two sounds it was enough to crack your nerves. When I went anywhere near her cage Chippy would watch me with an evil stare, and if I actually touched the cage she would charge toward my hand and I would have to be very quick in pulling it away to avoid getting bitten and clawed.

The thing that seemed to anger her more than anything else was to see me in possession of a hard-shelled nut, or even to catch the scent of one on my hands. Just to see me standing across the room with a nut in my hand was enough to put her into a frenzy and when I wanted to give her one through the bars she couldn't seem to understand that I was trying to give it to her rather than trying to take it away from her and she would run at me fiercely and try to snatch it out of my fingers with her claws. Finally the only way I could give her a nut was to pretend I was going to stick it through the bars up at the top of her cage—in that way tricking her into running up to the top—and then bend down quickly and stick it through at the bottom. And when she had the nut and had either buried it under the papers on the floor or had hidden it in her house, then it was just something more to defend. She wore herself out defending. She spent the better part of her days scurrying down to the bottom of her cage to guard the nuts on the floor and then scurrying back up to guard the ones in her house. At the end of a day she would be dead tired but even so when I stood near her cage after she had gone to bed she would know I was there and I would hear her clicking and moaning faintly.

Because of the way she attacked me whenever I touched her cage, I had to resort to wearing leather gloves when I cleaned it. Chippy didn't like the gloves. She was afraid of them. When she saw me putting them on she stopped everything and looked at them warily, and when I approached her with them on she ran around in her cage a couple of times and then disappeared abruptly into her house. I didn't like the gloves either. To me they were the symbol of the sad way my friendship with Chippy had turned out.

I couldn't help but agree with the idea I thought she was trying to get across—that it was time for her to go. It was only a question now of when I would release her and where. I spent a lot of time looking for a place where I thought Chippy would be happy, and finally I found what looked like a paradise for squirrels—a big private park that was full of a variety of trees, much like the property around my house. There were no cats in the park and no hunters were allowed in it either, so I thought that Chippy would not only be happy there but safe as well. I got permission from the authorities in charge of the park to release a squirrel on the grounds, and I even went so far as to scout out a location within the park that I thought Chippy would find particularly pleasant.

But August passed and September came and Chippy was still with me. I couldn't seem to bring myself to go through the actual motions of taking her out and letting her go. It was always tomorrow. I was always telling myself that I knew perfectly well it had to be done and that doubtless the sooner it was done the better for both of us, so I always said tomorrow without fail. Then tomorrow would come and there would always be some good reason why I couldn't do it. Part of it was sentimentality, part of it was indecision, and part of it was probably plain laziness. Anyway, the days kept going by and all I seemed to be able to do was say tomorrow definitely.

Twenty-two

Then one morning—it was the twelfth of September and the time was around nine o'clock—I got up from the table where I had been writing and put on my gloves and picked up Chippy's cage and carried her in it out of the house and all the way across the field and put it down in the shade of a gigantic oak whose lower branches swooped down so low that they brushed the top of it.

Chippy was a very shocked little squirrel. And I must admit that I was shocked, too, at my own precipitateness. I had made up my mind all of a sudden that this was the day and this was the moment, and there had been no time to go to the park or to think better of it because something had told me that if I didn't do it now I would never do it.

It was a fine morning. The sun was bright. There were

only a few clouds in the sky. It seemed to me that I had picked an ideal day to return Chippy to her own world.

I was sweating and out of breath from having carried the cage so far and so fast. I hadn't stopped once all the way. Chippy lay flat along one of her cross-branches, holding onto it tightly and looking apprehensive. I could tell she had decided that since she hadn't the faintest idea of what was going on the best thing for her to do was to go into a deep freeze and wait to see what developed. I stood close to the cage, looking at Chippy and letting it sink in that this was the last time we would be together, and perhaps it was only my imagination but I thought that she looked particularly handsome that morning. Her face was close to the bars and I reached my finger through and stroked her nose and scratched behind her ears. For the first time in a long while she didn't click or moan at me or try to bite. I began to feel sorry for her because I knew that she was frightened and that she was probably going to be a lot more frightened pretty soon when she was all on her own up in the trees. I started wondering if she had eaten anything that morning or if she was going away on an empty stomach, and then I thought about how much I was going to miss her even though she was as mean as a rattlesnake to me all the time—and then, knowing myself as I did and not putting it past myself for a minute that if I thought long enough about what I was doing I would in the end pick up the cage and carry it back into the house, I made the act I had begun complete and final and irrevocable by opening the door of the cage.

I suppose I thought that as soon as Chippy saw that the door was open she would run out. She didn't. She just kept on lying on her branch not moving so much as a whisker. I stood back and waited for a while and when she still didn't do anything I sat down on the grass and waited some more. After a long time she suddenly stirred and seemed to pull herself together. But instead of coming out of the door, she went down to the grass at the bottom of her cage. She had never had any experience of grass out in a field like that before and I could tell that the smells were fabulous by the eager way she ran around on it and stuck her nose down deep and snuffled in it.

She kept on fussing in the grass until some blue jays began scolding in the tree above us. Then she ran up and checked the nuts in her house, and after that she finally seemed to think it was time for her to face the fact that the door of her cage was open. I really think that she had been aware of it all along but had wanted time to try to figure out what it meant. The whole thing puzzled her. You could see that. That she had been abruptly transported here to a place where she had never been before was mystery enough. That I should have opened her door when it clearly implied that if she went through it she would be free was beyond her. She was distrustful. I think she truly suspected that there would be serious consequences if she left her cage now.

She hesitated for several minutes, perched on a cross-branch and gazing out through the open door, and then she came out. She clung to the side of the cage and hesitated again, looking back over her shoulder at me. Then she climbed on up to the top.

It was an electric moment. Chippy moved cautiously across the top of the cage toward the nearest oak branch. When she reached it she stood up on her hind legs and took a twig of it in her hands and bit the edge of a leaf and sniffed the bark. It was clear that for the first time she began to understand the meaning of what was happening to her. She was free. There were no bars around her. No walls. There was nothing above her but the sky and

137

what must have seemed to her like the great heavenly city of the branches and foliage of the trees that towered overhead.

She climbed onto the branch and ran along it. The farther she ran the faster she went. When she reached the immense trunk of the tree she ran around it twice, sideways, the way squirrels do. Then she came back along the branch toward me and stopped when she was close and looked down at me, through the leaves, and looking back up at her I had a funny feeling because seeing her there in the tree it occurred to me that she could have been any squirrel. She looked like any other one. Nothing about her marked her as a very special squirrel, my own squirrel, the one I had saved from a cat and had brought up in my house.

I thought that she looked at me in an impudent way, as if to say, "Why don't you try to get me back into that cage now? Why don't you try to get me to jump down on your shoulder? And see all the good it does you?"

She turned away suddenly and ran back to the trunk of the tree, and then she put on a startling exhibition. She ran like a streak all the way up to the top of the tree and then all the way back down again. And then she ran up again and started flinging herself around in the very highest branches. Watching her, very small up there in the sunlight, I was positive that she was going to slip and fall the whole way down and break her neck. I wanted to yell at her to take it easy, not to be so damn smart, to stop showing off because she wasn't impressing anybody anyway.

And then, when I saw that she wasn't going to fall, that she was as good at climbing and leaping from branch to branch as any squirrel that had spent its whole life in the trees, my attitude changed, and I began to feel proud of her. In a way it was like the model airplanes of my youth. I used to spend weeks putting together little airplanes made of balsam and tissue paper and glue that were supposed to fly and when finally the great day came when one of them was finished and I took it out to see if it would fly and it did, the feeling was stupendous. The thing that I had built with my own hands was good. It worked. And Chippy, the squirrel that I had raised with my own hands, was good. She worked. And watching her sail around up there, I began to realize fully how wrong it had been of me to have kept her away from the trees as long as I had. What a poor substitute for a tree I was. What a pathetic substitute for the whole outdoors my house was.

While all of this was going on, a certain movement in the distance caught my eye. A squirrel had come out on a limb of an oak tree two down from the one Chippy was playing in. It just lay on the limb for a few minutes and then it began working its way toward her. I had often thought about this, wondered what it would be like, Chippy's first encounter with a wild squirrel in the wild.

The squirrel kept coming. I walked a little way toward him and he passed by above me on a low limb. He was a big buck squirrel with a notch about two inches long out of his tail. I looked back up at Chippy and saw that she had noticed the other squirrel. She seemed very interested in him and came down her tree and went toward him on a limb that was intertwined with the limb that he was running on toward her.

As they approached each other, I thought, "My God, she hasn't even been out here fifteen minutes yet and she's already having her first date!"

But what happened next was not what I had anticipated. The two squirrels closed in a rush right above me and there were piercing squeals followed by furious action as they chased each other like whirlwinds around and around on the limb. Then one of them broke free and ran away in a general southerly direction, with the other in hot pursuit. There was another brief skirmish and more squeals, another chase through a royal poinciana, and then one of the squirrels suddenly dropped about twenty feet to the ground.

They were quite far away and I couldn't tell which one of them had fallen, but I knew that it had to be Chippy.

The poinciana tree was on the adjoining piece of property and I couldn't go directly over there because the underbrush was very dense along the low stone wall that marked the property line. So I ran out my gate and down the road to the next gate. What I expected to find as I hurried toward the poinciana was a battered, broken, perhaps even bloody, furry body lying crumpled on the ground. What I actually found was Chippy standing up on her hind legs and watching me curiously as I came pounding across the lawn. When I caught sight of her I stopped. There seemed to be nothing at all wrong with her. In fact, she looked as if she had probably been snuffling and digging in the grass and having a fine time before she had heard me coming. The other squirrel was nowhere to be seen.

I wanted her to get back up into the tree because I was afraid that a cat might stroll by at any moment and catch her. So I went toward her slowly, trying to shoo her toward the poinciana by making little pushing motions with my hands. She kept on staring at me for a moment, and then she suddenly started running toward me. I didn't know what to do, so I retreated quickly. At that, Chippy turned around and raced back to the tree. In an instant she was up on a limb looking down at me. Then she headed back toward my side of the wall and I lost sight of her.

When I returned to the place where I had left the cage, I saw Chippy running around in the big oak again. I thought that it might be a good idea to stay out there with her for a while so that she would know that I was still very much with her in spirit even though she was technically no longer my squirrel, so I went back to the house and got a chaise longue and set it up in the field in the shade of the oaks and sat down to watch her in comfort. Pretty soon she got tired of playing and began an enthusiastic investigation of the huge and exciting new world around her. I could see her sampling a twig here and a leaf there and getting absorbed in something wonderful that she had discovered and then abruptly dashing away somewhere else, like a tourist who wants to see everything at once. Sometimes I would lose her and have to go over and walk around under the tree looking up until I sighted her again. A couple of times she came all the way down the trunk to the base of the tree and started digging in the good mulchy earth around the roots. On those occasions I had no choice but to chase her back up the tree because that was a habit I definitely didn't want her getting into, at least until she had learned to look out for cats.

After I had chased her up she always came and looked down at me from a limb over my head, and those were times when more than ever before I wished that I could talk to her, because there were several things that I really wanted to say. First, of course, I would have tried to impress on her the importance of being on the lookout for owls, hawks, and cats. Next, I would have told her to be very cautious at first in her relationships with other squirrels, to remember that the kind of life that she had led so far was very different from the kind of life that they led and therefore there were many things that she knew about that they didn't but that there were also lots of things that they knew about that she didn't.

Then I would have told her that she wouldn't have to worry too much right in the beginning about where the next meal was coming from, because for the first week or so I planned to come out to the tree a couple of times a day and visit with her and bring her all of the things that she liked and which of course she wouldn't be able to find out there. Not that I intended to keep it up forever. Just until she got settled and learned her way around. After that she would be strictly on her own.

But most important of all from the short-term point of view, I would have told her that it seemed to me that she should start thinking right away about making her nest, because while I knew that it was great fun doing what she was doing I also knew that picking out a good spot for a nest and then actually constructing it would take a lot of time and I didn't want her to spend the whole day gadding about and then suddenly realize half an hour before sunset that she didn't have a place to lay down her head—because if there was one thing I knew about her it was that she was a squirrel who liked a nice cosy nest to curl up in at night.

But of course I couldn't say any of that to her. All I could do was hope that she would try to use her head a little bit about things now that she was on her own.

As the morning wore on I began to see more squirrels. They would just appear out of nowhere in the tree where Chippy was and it became more and more difficult all the time for me to figure out which of them was her. I would follow a squirrel for a while thinking that it was Chippy and then change my mind and think that it really didn't look much like her at all and start following another one that seemed to look just like her and go through the same thing again a little later. Finally I went over to the tree to get a closer look at a squirrel that had come down on a low branch and that I was confident was Chippy but just wanted to check on to be quite certain about and found that it was actually a young male. After that I stood under the tree looking up and feeling that I had really lost Chippy now. She could have been that squirrel sitting motionless on that dead branch up there or that one being chased along a limb by an angry mockingbird over there. Or she might not have been any of these squirrels at all but have long since traveled far away and out of my sight altogether. So I gave up watching for her and went back to the house.

Twenty-three

The first thing I noticed when I came back in from the field and entered the living room was that the cage wasn't there. It was the first time in more than a year that I had come into the room and not seen it and the room looked empty without it.

I set to work right away cleaning up the papers on the floor where the cage had been because I wanted to get the whole thing over with and when that was done that would be the end of it. After I had finished the job I found myself standing in the middle of the room with three pecans and two brazil nuts in my hand that I had discovered hidden in the papers, and for just a moment there I didn't know quite what to do with them. Ordinarily I would have put them back into the cage when I put down the fresh papers, but now of course there was not going to be any of that any more. Finally I just tossed the nuts into the waste paper basket—and for the first time I let it come home to me how nice it was going to be not to be a small-time zoo keeper any more. I felt liberated. And the more I thought about it the more liberated I felt.

And there was so much more to rejoice about besides. Best of all was the fact that I wouldn't have to worry about Chippy any longer—whether she was happy, whether she was bored, whether she was eating the right food, whether she was getting enough exercise, and what in God's name I would do if she ever got sick again.

Beyond that was the spiritual side of the thing. I wouldn't have to torture myself any longer about whether it was right to keep Chippy in my house. And the social side. I wouldn't have to be so self-conscious any more, always suspecting that people were probably thinking that it was preposterous, absurd and just plain screwy for a grown man to have gotten himself so fantastically involved with a little squirrel.

And from Chippy's point of view being set free obviously was sheer heaven. She had never looked so happy in her life as she had out there in the trees. And there was no longer any real question in my mind that she wouldn't be able to make it. As a matter of fact I thought she would do just fine. Certainly there was no shortage of good things to eat. And she was a little over a year old and big and strong and healthy. Hadn't she already had her first fight with another squirrel and survived it? And I thought that when it came right down to it she would be smart enough to stay away from cats.

The whole thing seemed to be all so much to the good that I felt like having a celebration. So I got a bottle of beer out of the icebox and sat in the living room drinking it and feeling liberated. And if the room seemed empty without the cage, that was just an illusion. And if I kept glancing at the place where it had stood to see what Chippy was doing, that was just a habit. And if I felt a little lonely, I would soon get over it.

When I finished the beer I went over to my desk and took up my work where I had left off after suddenly deciding to take Chippy out to the trees. But it wasn't long before I began to feel restless and thought that I would take a short break and run down to the village and check the morning mail.

As I was walking down the driveway to my car I couldn't help looking across the field toward the oak trees. Then I paused, seeing a squirrel in one of the trees and wondering if it was Chippy. I walked across the field trying to keep my eye on the squirrel, but by the time I had come up close to the tree that I had seen it in it had vanished. I looked around but didn't see any other squirrels anywhere and so I continued on to my car and went down to the village. When I came back I glanced over at the trees on my way to the house but this time I didn't stop or go over to them.

I had lunch and worked until about three o'clock. Then I decided to take a walk outside and inevitably found myself drawn to the oaks. It was still a fine sunny day but very hot. The shade had changed and my chaise was in the sun now, so I moved it back into the shade of the oaks and sat down again. As I sat looking up at the trees a squirrel would appear now and then. Sometimes they were foreign squirrels traveling through the property on their way from somewhere to somewhere but usually they were just the local squirrels looking for acorns. A few acorns had appeared so far on the oaks but from the size of them I knew that it would not be a good year. The acorns of live oaks are never very big but some years they are not much bigger than peas and then again some years there are simply none at all.

The afternoon grew hotter and drowsier. There were many birds all around me—blue jays and cardinals and mourning doves—all poking about in the grass looking for acorns that had fallen. Once in a while the doves would panic for no reason that you could see and fly away with their wings beating hard to lift their heavy bodies off the ground. Hummingbirds worked in the flowers nearby, and fat green insects whose name I have never known hovered glistening in the sunlight low over the field. Occasionally something would stir far back in the thick underbrush along the wall and I would guess that it was the foxes. Lately a pair of beautiful gray foxes had taken up residence on the property. I never saw them except late at night and early in the morning. At night I would suddenly have them in my headlights when I came home and my lights swept across the field as the car turned in the driveway. In the morning I would always see them in a certain little clearing where the sun slanted down through the trees. When I saw them the male would usually be sitting on his haunches with his nose lifted straight up to smell the wind for danger while the little female washed his face and throat with her tongue.

The cage was still where I had set it down, and I wasn't quite sure what to do about it. What I had hoped was that after Chippy had made her nest in the tree she would come down and take the nuts out of her house and store them in it. Now I realized what a truly crazy idea that had been—to seriously think that as soon as Chippy was set free she would go to work organizing her new life. I was sure that right now building a nest was the farthest thing from her mind and that the chances of her coming anywhere near her cage again were remote. Still, I thought that I would leave the cage where it was for the time being.

Suddenly I saw a branch of a holly tree off to my right dip down as if a weight had been put on it and I knew that either a bird had lit on it or a squirrel had run out near the end of it. I walked down that way and I saw the branch dip again as I came near the tree. The tree was actually more like a big bush and it was part of a clump of holly trees with long low-drooping branches that grew between the oaks and the stone wall that ran along beside the roadway. I was partly blinded by the bright sunlight after the deep shade of the oaks and as I leaned forward, squinting and trying to see into the dark green leaves, a squirrel's face appeared right in front of me. It stared at me and I was startled and stood looking back at it for a minute, and then I knew that it was Chippy. Both of us, I think, were quite dumbfounded at seeing each other up that close again. Finally I opened my mouth and started to say something, but just then Chippy disappeared.

I saw her again a moment later in the next holly tree and she seemed to be working her way on down toward the road. I absolutely gave up on her then. That she had left the nice big safe oaks to go scrounging around in the holly and possibly even to go out to the road and try to cross it was proof as far as I was concerned that she had definitely decided not to use her head at all.

So I went back to the house and worked again for a while, until I felt a sudden breeze from the west blow through the living room. The breeze was cold and I went to the window to look out and saw something that rather alarmed me. The whole sky to the west was dark and full of lightning. I went outside to get a better look at it and saw that an evil-looking front was filling up the sky rapidly. This was something that I hadn't counted on because the weather had been fair for more than a week and I had thought that it would continue that way for at least a few more days.

For a while after that, as the afternoon went by, I still hoped that, as so often happens in September, the storm would advance just so far and then meet resistance from the air above the coastline and in the end stand back and turn itself loose over the Everglades. But it kept coming and around six o'clock there was lightning and thunder and another strong gust of wind and a brief preliminary flurry of rain.

I went back across the field then, thinking that if I knew my squirrel, when she had heard the thunder and had felt the first cold drops of rain on her nose, she might have had an abrupt change of heart about the charms of nature and instinctively made a beeline for her cage and the security of her house. But when I reached the cage I found it empty and no sign of Chippy around anywhere.

That posed a new problem. I felt there was a good chance that Chippy would want to go to her house if the storm got very bad, yet I was afraid that if she did come down from the trees and get into her house she would be easy game for a cat. I could see it clearly. Some cat wandering around in the field, comes upon the cage, smells squirrel all over it, climbs up the side of the cage, slips through the open door and catches Chippy asleep in her house.

The answer was to close the door and fasten it securely with clothespins. But then I could see Chippy in the midst of the storm running frantically all over the outside of the cage, trying to find a way in. Or I could have taken the cage away altogether. But I didn't want to do that because, I guess, I wanted Chippy to see that the cage remained there and for her to sense from that that if it turned out finally that she couldn't make it in the wild and she wanted to come back home she always could.

I compromised by getting an old yellow slicker out of

my car and putting it over the top of the cage to keep out the rain and deciding that I would leave the door open until late that night anyway.

It was getting dark by then. I walked back and forth under the oaks calling, "Chippy, Chippy," although I really didn't know what I was calling her for. Soon it began raining harder and I had to go back to the house.

I went out three or four times that night with an umbrella and a flashlight to look in the cage, but Chippy never was there. At about midnight I went out for the last time and locked up the cage. After I went to bed the storm got ferocious and the way the wind was driving the rain against the windows it sounded almost like a hurricane. I couldn't help thinking, lying there and listening to it, that ordinarily it was on nights like this that Chippy got in her best sleeping, all curled up warm and snug in her house with her tail pulled around her.

Twenty-four

I got up early the next morning and went outside and across the field as soon as I had had my first cup of coffee. The storm was over but a little rain was still falling and the air was misty, and the mosquitoes were out in vast numbers.

I looked around for Chippy for several minutes, batting at the mosquitoes, and even called her name a few times, but I didn't see her, or any other squirrels for that matter. Then the mosquitoes got to be too much and I had to go back inside.

I went looking for Chippy again later on that morning and again after lunch, and it was when I had come back to the house the second time that I realized that it was over, that Chippy apparently was going to make it on the outside after all, that I probably would never see her again, and that it was time for me to stop worrying about her now. So I put her out of my mind and went to work. I worked steadily most of the afternoon and when I had to go down to the village at one point I didn't even look out across the field.

Just before dark I went out again and again I didn't look over at the trees on my way to my car or on my way back from it. But as I was passing along a section of the driveway that was densely overhung by the branches of fruit trees, something caught my eye. I don't know why it did. It never should have. It certainly didn't stand out like a beacon in the gloom. It certainly didn't even so much as twitch a whisker to attract my attention. But I did happen to see it somehow. It was off to my left, stretched out on a low branch of a sapodilla that had been snapped off in a hurricane two years before. It was a squirrel.

I stopped and went toward it cautiously, trying to get close enough to see it clearly in that bad light. It immediately occurred to me that it was Chippy, but it didn't look like Chippy. I saw it in profile. It lay with its hands tucked under its chin and its chin resting on the branch and its tail laid out flat on the branch behind it. I had a feeling that something tragic had happened, that the squirrel must have fallen from high up in the tree and broken its back or its legs and had dragged itself up onto that branch to die.

I went a little closer to it and it still didn't move. But I thought I saw its shiny eye studying me. Its fur was wet and its tail matted and all in all it was the most bedraggled-looking squirrel I had ever seen. I leaned closer, and suddenly it turned its face toward me, and in that instant I knew that it was Chippy.

"Chips?" I said.

She just continued to look at me.

I looked back at her, trying to figure out what she was doing lying there on that branch that way all wet and not even looking anything like herself. And then it came to me that the sapodilla tree was about halfway between the oak trees and my house and that perhaps Chippy had been trying to make her way home through the trees and had gotten this far and then had stopped here hoping that I would come by and take her the rest of the way.

But maybe that wasn't it at all. Maybe she was there just because she happened to be there. Because if she had wanted to be seen, why hadn't she made herself a little more obvious? Why had she lurked over there on the branch as still as a mouse so that it was just by a miracle that I happened to see her.

"Do you want to come home, Chippy?" I said.

Which was like expecting an answer from the Sphinx.

Then I had an idea and I went across the field and lugged the cage back with me to the sapodilla tree and set it down where Chippy could jump over onto it if she wanted. I opened the door and waited. For a minute she didn't do anything. Then she jumped onto my shoulder and ran down the back of my shirt and my pantsleg to the ground and squatted and made a little puddle. After that she ran back up to my shoulder and hopped from there into the cage, and I picked up the cage and took her home.